CROCK·POT®
◆ THE ORIGINAL SLOW COOKER ◆

diabetic
recipes

Publications International, Ltd.

Nutritional Analysis: Jacqueline B. Marcus, M.S., R.D., L.D., C.N.S., F.A.D.A.

Every effort has been made to check the accuracy of the nutritional information that appears with each recipe. However, because numerous variables account for a wide range of values for certain foods, nutritive analyses in this book should be considered approximate. Different results may be obtained by using different nutrient databases and different brand-name products.

Crock-Pot® and the Crock-Pot® logo are registered trademarks of Sunbeam Products, Inc. used under license.

Some of the products listed in this publication may be in limited distribution.

This book is for informational purposes and is not intended to provide medical advice. Neither Publications International, Ltd., nor the authors, editors or publisher takes responsibility for any possible consequences from any treatment, procedure, exercise, dietary modification, action, or applications of medication or preparation by any person reading or following the information in this cookbook. The publication of this book does not constitute the practice of medicine, and this cookbook does not replace your physician, pharmacist or health-care specialist. Before undertaking any course of treatment or nutritional plan, the authors, editors and publisher advise the reader to check with a physician or other health-care provider.

Not all recipes in this cookbook are appropriate for all people with diabetes. Health-care providers, registered dietitians and certified diabetes educators can help design specific meal plans tailored to individual needs.

Photography on pages 17, 27, 33, 65, 71, 77, 79, 96, 101, 103, 105, 111, 114, 115, 122, 127, 128, 139, 143, 149, 158, 159, 160, 163, 165, 169, 171, 173, 175, 177, 178, 179, 183, 195, 207, 220, 223, 227, 233 and 239 by PIL Photo Studio.
Photographer: Tate Hunt
Photographer's Assistant: Justin Paris
Prop Stylist: Paula Walters
Food Stylists: Kathy Joy, Mary Ann Melone
Assistant Food Stylists: Lissa Levy, Breana Moeller

Pictured on the front cover (*clockwise from top left*): White Bean Chili (page 129), Black Bean Stuffed Peppers (page 183), Sweet Chicken Curry (page 144), Oatmeal with Maple Glazed Apples and Cranberries (page 20), Pork Roast with Dijon Tarragon Glaze (page 114), Greek Lemon and Rice Soup (page 52), Mu Shu Turkey (page 156) and Slow Cooker Veggie Stew (page 182).

Pictured on the back cover (*clockwise from top left*): Cran-Orange Acorn Squash (page 210), Rustic Vegetable Soup (page 48), Spicy Asian Pork Filling (page 124), French Carrot Medley (page 244), Apple-Cherry Glazed Pork Chops (page 102), Peppered Pork Cutlets with Onion Gravy (page 100), Southwestern Beans and Vegetables (page 179), Ratatouille with Parmesan Cheese (page 164), Sweet Potato & Pecan Casserole (page 206) and Roast Tomato-Basil Soup (page 33).

ISBN-13: 978-1-4508-2409-5
ISBN-10: 1-4508-2409-9

Library of Congress Control Number: 2011922388

Manufactured in China.

8 7 6 5 4 3 2 1

Table of Contents

p. 16

p. 100

p. 225

Slow Cooking the Healthy Way

CROCK-POT® slow cookers have been a source of favorite family meals for many years, and while you may have diabetes, you still can enjoy some of the classic comfort foods you've always loved. In fact, plenty of recipes that have always been made in a **CROCK-POT®** slow cooker can easily fit within a diabetic meal plan.

With a little guidance, you can continue to eat your favorite foods—just with a healthy twist. Whether you are newly diagnosed or have been living with diabetes for years, you can use this book to re-invent some of the best hearty, homestyle dishes.

Knowledge Is Power

In order to manage your diabetes, it's important that you understand what causes your disease and why the foods you eat play an important role in its control and treatment.

There are two types of diabetes mellitus: type 1 insulin-dependent diabetes mellitus, (also known as juvenile diabetes), and type 2 diabetes mellitus, (formerly known as non-insulin dependent diabetes mellitus or adult-onset diabetes mellitus). While the causes of these diseases are different, the role that food plays in your management of each disease is the same.

Deciphering the Terms

After we consume a meal, the foods we eat are broken down during digestion into glucose. This is important because the energy we need to live comes from the glucose in our bodies. Glucose provides the power for every body function, whether it's walking, lifting weights or sleeping. The term "blood glucose" is often used interchangeably with "blood sugar," as glucose is a simple form of sugar.

Excess glucose that isn't used for energy right away is stored in the muscle, liver and fat tissues for later use. Insulin is a hormone that is responsible for taking the glucose that has been released into the bloodstream after digestion and storing it into the muscle, liver and fat cells.

For those with type 1 diabetes, the pancreas is not able to produce insulin; consequently, blood glucose produced by digestion continues to circulate in the bloodstream. In type 2 diabetes, the pancreas produces insulin but the muscle, liver and fat cells that should accept the glucose from insulin do not function properly and will not take in what is circulating in the blood. The glucose then remains within the bloodstream. This is known as "insulin resistance."

Living With Diabetes

Increased levels of blood glucose can cause serious medical complications, including excessive thirst, hunger, blurred vision, weight loss and dehydration. In fact, these symptoms typically lead someone to consult a physician and ultimately to their medical diagnosis.

Medicine often plays a role in diabetes maintenance. People with type 1 diabetes cannot produce insulin themselves, so they require an intravenous pump or injections to provide the insulin needed to transfer glucose from the blood to the cells. Some people with type 2 diabetes also require supplemental insulin and many take drugs to assist in the upload of glucose from the blood to the tissues.

Although medical treatment varies from person to person, diet is a major component in the treatment plan for anyone with diabetes. The best way to educate yourself about the disease and its treatment is to consult with your physician, a registered dietitian and/or a Certified Diabetes Educator to create an individualized diabetic meal plan that suits your physical requirements and your lifestyle. You will then be able to make responsible choices and still take pleasure in eating the dishes you have always treasured.

Food Basics

Whether you are dealing with type 1 or type 2 diabetes, it's important to be aware of exactly what and how much you're eating. It's also crucial to know the effects that various foods have on your blood glucose levels.

The fuel that our bodies use as energy is Calories. Calories come from four main sources—carbohydrates, protein, fat and alcohol—and each of these sources affects your blood glucose levels differently. In addition, most foods are not comprised of only fat or only carbohydrates; thus, it's important to look at the Nutrition Facts Panel on a package or the nutrition information listed on a menu or recipe to be sure of exactly what you're eating. We will be looking only at the nutrients that pertain to the recipes in this book—carbohydrates, protein and fat.

Carbohydrates are the primary nutrient found in breads, pasta and cereals, and they make up approximately half of the calories we consume. Carbohydrates are also the greatest contributor to our blood glucose levels. If someone were to consume a piece of white bread, he or she would experience a spike in blood glucose levels soon after. This is because our digestive process breaks down carbohydrates easily and rapidly.

Often, people with diabetes try to control their disease by restricting the amount of carbohydrates they consume. However, eliminating food groups is never a good idea—control of the disease comes from knowing what types of foods to eat and which nutrients to look out for.

Your protein consumption should also be considered. Protein—found in lean meats, fish, soy, fat-free or low-fat dairy products, beans and nuts—is digested comparatively slowly. As a result, eating foods with a significant amount of protein makes us feel full sooner and satisfied longer after we eat. Additionally, when protein is eaten with carbohydrates, the protein delays the blood glucose response.

There is a lot of speculation on where fat fits within the diet. For many years fat was considered to be bad, something to be restricted, but this is not necessarily true. While fat does contribute more calories than equivalent amounts of

Substituting Good Fats for Bad Fats

1. *Cook with olive oil.* If you need flavorless oil, try canola or grapeseed oil. If the recipe requires the rich taste of butter, you can usually replace half of it with oil without compromising the flavor.
2. *Prepare it yourself.* Store-bought salad dressings and sauces can be loaded with sugar, sodium and preservatives. Make a simple vinaigrette or marinade with olive oil, or just pass a good quality vinegar and olive oil at the table.
3. *Avoid processed meat.* It is not only loaded with sodium, it may also be high in fat.
4. *Choose low-fat dairy.* Drink low-fat milk and cook with low-fat dairy products. Watch out for cheese, as it can contribute to a lot of saturated, or

"bad," fat to your diet. Try using small amounts of full-flavored cheeses like Parmesan or feta.
5. *Cook at home.* It is no secret that foods prepared at restaurants are not good for us; they're loaded with hidden ingredients and the portion sizes are huge! Eating out makes us take in higher amounts of fat, carbohydrates, sodium and calories.

carbohydrates or protein, certain types of fat have been proven to have health benefits.

The types of fats to limit are saturated fats and trans fats, commonly found in butter, cheeses, meats and other animal products. These types of fats have been found to increase levels of LDL cholesterol (the "bad" cholesterol) in the body and therefore are strongly connected to your risk of heart disease. On the other hand, mono-unsaturated fats and poly-unsaturated fats—present in sources such as avocados, vegetable oils and fish—have been found to improve heart health by decreasing LDL cholesterol levels in the body, as well as reducing inflammation.

Despite the popularity of a "fat-free" diet, there is clearly no need to eliminate fat, but to watch the type and amount consumed, as it's a large source of calories. Replace foods in your diet that may be high in saturated or trans fats with those that are higher in unsaturated fats. For example, sauté your vegetables in olive oil instead of butter, and replace some meat with fish that is higher in unsaturated fats, such as salmon.

The Facts of Fiber

Dietary fiber is a key component to the success of any diet. Fiber has been proven effective in disease prevention, weight loss and blood glucose control. It's naturally present in plants and therefore is a major nutritional component of fruits, vegetables, beans, nuts, seeds and whole grains. In fact, dietary fiber is what leaves us feeling satisfied after we eat a large apple or a mixed vegetable salad.

Dietary fiber slows down the process of digestion, which helps in a couple of ways. First, our brains get time to decide we're full and signal us to stop eating. Additionally, by delaying the digestive process, dietary fiber slows down the breakdown of food to glucose, moderating the blood glucose rise that occurs after any meal.

There are two forms of dietary fiber that you may see on food labels—insoluble and soluble fiber. While both are classified as fiber, their benefits differ.

Most of the fiber we consume is insoluble fiber. This type of fiber increases the weight and size of your stool, which allows regular bowel movements to occur, preventing constipation and aiding in digestive health. (If you want to increase fiber in your diet, just be cautious not to add too much too quickly or increase the amount of fiber in your diet without increasing your water intake, as well. A drastic increase of fiber in the diet can cause abdominal discomfort, gas and constipation.)

Soluble fiber also has significant health benefits. This type of fiber—found mostly in beans, oats and the peels of apples—absorbs water. This absorption provides a feeling of fullness as you eat, which helps you avoid overeating. This type of fiber also slows down the digestive processes, again helping to delay the blood glucose response after a meal.

High Fiber Fruits and Vegetables (per 1-cup, unless otherwise indicated)

Avocado, cubed	10g
Green Peas	9g
Raspberries	8g
Acorn Squash	6g
Pear, large with skin	6g
Apple, large with skin	5g
Corn	5g
Potato, medium, baked with skin	5g
Asparagus	4g
Carrot	4g
Orange	4g
Spinach, cooked	4g
Strawberries	4g
Banana, medium	3g
Broccoli	2g
Grapefruit, ½ of whole fruit	2g

Five Easy Ways to Increase the Fiber in Your Diet

1. *Start out strong.* Choose a high fiber hot cereal with fruit for breakfast.
2. *Switch to whole grains.* Try brown rice, whole grain pastas and breads.
3. *Eat the whole fruit.* The fiber is in the peel and the pulp.
4. *Drop the peeler.* Instead, scrub apples and potatoes and cook with the peel on.
5. *Get big on beans.* Eat beans or lentils three times a week. They're loaded with fiber.

Soluble fiber plays an important role in heart health, too. When bound to water, soluble fiber forms a gel-like substance in the digestive tract. In this form, it absorbs cholesterol, which is then carried out of the body. This reduces your blood cholesterol levels, helping to reduce your risk of heart disease.

Both types of dietary fiber play an important role in weight loss. Insoluble fiber increases the bulk in our stomach, while soluble fiber slows down the digestive processes. As a result, we feel fuller from a smaller amount of food for an extended period of time.

While many processed food products do have some added fiber, the best sources are natural, unrefined foods such as fruits, vegetables, whole grains and beans—common ingredients in many of the recipes in this book.

Putting It All Together

In a nutshell, carbohydrates break down easily during digestion. When you eat something high in carbohydrates, your blood glucose will rise quickly. Fat and protein also break down into glucose, but they'll go through many more steps at the cellular level before this occurs, and thus don't cause the spike in blood glucose levels that carbohydrates do. In fact, when carbohydrates are eaten along with some protein or fat, the blood glucose response is delayed.

Most people are much more likely to eat a food or a meal that consists of a combination of carbohydrates, protein and fat than of a single nutrient alone. Therefore, paying attention to each of these elements within a meal will assist in blood glucose control.

For example, when you eat a turkey sandwich, the protein from the turkey will delay the response that the carbohydrates in the bread would normally have on blood glucose levels if eaten alone. (To delay the response further, eat whole wheat bread, full of dietary fiber, which will leave you feeling full and satisfied until your next meal.)

Portion Distortion

Regardless of what you're eating, one of the most important things that you should pay attention to is portion size. Whether your guide is the serving size listed on the Nutrition Facts Panel on any packaged food or the nutrition information listed at the bottom of the recipes in this book, portion size is always pertinent.

For instance, you may pour yourself a bowl of cereal with milk for breakfast. Ideally, you also may see that the serving size listed on the Nutrition Facts Panel is 1 cup—but chances are, the amount of cereal in your bowl is not 1 cup. Additionally, the amount of milk that you added to that cereal will need to be considered if you want to know, for example, how many total calories were in that bowl of cereal. Learning to recognize all of the ingredients in a dish and the recommended serving sizes are fundamental tools to the success of any diet.

Portion control is particularly crucial for people with diabetes in order to maintain their blood glucose levels within a healthy range. Many people with diabetes will focus on their carbohydrate amounts and space their consumption throughout the day. This type of meal plan will help to prevent large spikes in blood glucose levels, as the goal for managing diabetes is to keep your blood glucose levels at a steady, consistent level at all times.

A Healthy Way of Life

This book is a guide and a resource for helping you create some of your favorite dishes in your **CROCK-POT®** slow cooker and fit them into a healthy meal plan. The nutrition information is provided with each recipe in this book so that you'll be aware of how each dish will affect your blood glucose levels and fit within your diabetic diet. The nutrition information listed is based on a single serving and does not include garnishes or optional ingredients; when a range is given for an ingredient, the nutritional analysis reflects the lesser amount. Please consult a registered dietitian or health care provider who can offer nutrition advice, tips and meal plans that are all specific to you, your health condition and your lifestyle.

Tips for Adding Veggies to Your Diet

1. *Make it easy on yourself.* Choose prewashed bags of vegetables or bring home goodies from the salad bar at the local supermarket.

2. *Go vegetarian once a week.* Plan a whole meal around a vegetable-based main dish. Try a soup, stew or pasta creation.

3. *Cook with more veggies.* Add veggies to your favorite dishes, like zucchini or carrots, in meat loaf or breads.

4. *Try something new and different.* Add color and flavor to your menus with less mainstream vegetables. Try mustard greens, beets or different varieties of more common veggies such as Italian-style green beans.

5. *Grow your own or shop locally.* Grow vegetables in your garden or visit a farmers' market or produce stand. You will be exposed to all different types of vegetables that you'll want to start cooking with. Plus, eating fresh fruits and vegetables is a great way to get your vitamins.

Breakfast Dishes

Breakfast Quinoa

- 1½ **cups quinoa**
- 3 **cups water**
- 3 **packed tablespoons brown sugar**
- 2 **tablespoons maple syrup**
- 1½ **teaspoons ground cinnamon**
- ¾ **cup golden raisins (optional)**
- **Sliced strawberries and banana**

1. Place quinoa in fine-mesh strainer; rinse well under cold running water. Transfer to **CROCK-POT®** slow cooker.

2. Stir in water, brown sugar, maple syrup and cinnamon. Cover; cook on LOW 5 hours or on HIGH 2½ hours or until quinoa is tender and water is absorbed.

3. Add raisins, if desired, for last 10 to 15 minutes of cooking time. Top quinoa with strawberries and banana.

Makes 6 servings

Nutrition Information

Calories.............................280
Total Fat..............................9g
Saturated Fat.......................2g
Protein 4g
Carbohydrate...................49g
Cholesterol....................25mg
Fiber....................................2g
Sodium..........................230mg

Dietary Exchanges:
1 Fruit, 1½ Starch, 1½ Fat,
½ Other

Tip

This recipe works best in round **CROCK-POT®** slow cookers.

Orange Cranberry-Nut Bread

Nonstick cooking spray
2 **cups all-purpose flour**
1 **teaspoon baking powder**
½ **teaspoon baking soda**
¼ **teaspoon salt**
½ **cup chopped pecans**
1 **cup dried cranberries**
2 **teaspoons dried orange peel**
⅔ **cup boiling water**
¾ **cup sugar**
2 **tablespoons shortening**
1 **egg, lightly beaten**
1 **teaspoon vanilla**

1. Coat 3-quart **CROCK-POT®** slow cooker with nonstick cooking spray. Blend flour, baking powder, baking soda and salt in medium bowl. Mix in pecans; set aside.

2. Combine cranberries and orange peel in separate medium bowl; pour boiling water over fruit mixture and stir. Add sugar, shortening, egg and vanilla; stir just until blended. Add flour mixture; stir just until blended.

3. Pour batter into **CROCK-POT®** slow cooker. Cover; cook on HIGH 1¼ to 1½ hours or until edges begin to brown and cake tester inserted into center comes out clean. Remove insert from **CROCK-POT®** slow cooker. Cool on wire rack about 10 minutes; remove bread from insert and cool completely on rack.

Makes 8 to 10 servings

Nutrition Information

Calories	238
Total Fat	7g
Saturated Fat	2g
Protein	8g
Carbohydrate	38g
Cholesterol	78mg
Fiber	2g
Sodium	154mg

Dietary Exchanges:
1 Fruit, 1 Starch, 1½ Fat

Note

To make foil handles: Tear off three 18×2-inch strips of heavy foil or use regular foil folded to double thickness. Crisscross foil strips in spoke design and place in slow cooker to allow for easy removal of bread pudding.

Luscious Pecan Bread Pudding

- 3 **cups day-old French bread cubes**
- 3 **tablespoons chopped pecans, toasted**
- 2¼ **cups low-fat (1%) milk**
- 2 **eggs, beaten**
- ½ **cup sugar**
- 1 **teaspoon vanilla**
- ¾ **teaspoon ground cinnamon, divided**
- ¾ **cup reduced-calorie cranberry juice cocktail**
- 1½ **cups frozen pitted tart cherries**
- 2 **tablespoons sugar substitute**

1. Toss bread cubes and pecans in soufflé dish. Combine milk, eggs, sugar, vanilla and ½ teaspoon cinnamon in large bowl. Pour over bread mixture in soufflé dish. Cover tightly with foil; make foil handles (see note).

2. Place soufflé dish in **CROCK-POT®** slow cooker. Pour hot water into **CROCK-POT®** slow cooker to about 1½ inches from top of soufflé dish. Cover; cook on LOW 2 to 3 hours.

3. Meanwhile, combine cranberry juice and remaining ¼ teaspoon cinnamon in small saucepan; stir in frozen cherries. Bring sauce to a boil over medium heat; cook about 5 minutes. Remove from heat. Stir in sugar substitute.

4. Lift soufflé dish from slow cooker with foil handles. Serve bread pudding with cherry sauce.

Makes 6 servings

Nutrition Information

Calories.............................298
Total Fat..............................12g
Saturated Fat.......................2g
Protein................................25g
Carbohydrate.....................23g
Cholesterol.....................43mg
Fiber......................................1g
Sodium..........................719mg

Dietary Exchanges:
1 Starch, 2 Meat, ½ Fat,
½ Milk

Sausage and Red Pepper Strata

Nonstick cooking spray

12 **ounces bulk reduced-fat breakfast pork sausage**

1 **teaspoon dried oregano**

½ **teaspoon red pepper flakes (optional)**

8 **slices day-old French bread, cut into ½-inch cubes**

1 **medium red bell pepper, finely chopped**

½ **cup chopped fresh parsley, plus additional for garnish**

2 **cups cholesterol-free egg substitute**

2 **cups evaporated skim milk**

2 **teaspoons Dijon mustard**

½ **teaspoon black pepper**

1 **cup (4 ounces) shredded reduced-fat sharp Cheddar cheese**

1. Spray large nonstick skillet with nonstick cooking spray; heat over medium-high heat. Add sausage, oregano and red pepper flakes, if desired; cook and stir until browned. Drain on paper towels.

2. Coat **CROCK-POT®** slow cooker with nonstick cooking spray. Add bread. Sprinkle sausage evenly over bread; top with bell pepper and parsley.

3. Combine egg substitute, milk, mustard and black pepper in medium bowl; whisk until well blended. Pour egg mixture evenly over sausage. Cover; cook on LOW 3 to 3½ hours or on HIGH 2 to 2½ hours or until eggs are firm but still moist.

4. Sprinkle cheese over top. Cover and let stand 5 minutes or until cheese is melted. Garnish with additional parsley.

Makes 8 servings

Nutrition Information

Calories.............................230
Total Fat................................4g
Saturated Fat......................1g
Protein 6g
Carbohydrate...................47g
Cholesterol.....................3mg
Fiber.......................................6g
Sodium...........................158mg

Dietary Exchanges:
1 Fruit, 2 Starch, ½ Fat

Oatmeal with Maple Glazed Apples and Cranberries

3 **cups water**

2 **cups uncooked quick-cooking or old-fashioned oats**

¼ **teaspoon salt**

1 **teaspoon unsalted butter**

2 **medium red or golden delicious apples, unpeeled, cut into ½-inch chunks**

¼ **teaspoon ground cinnamon**

2 **tablespoons sugar-free maple syrup**

4 **tablespoons dried cranberries**

1. Combine water, oats and salt in **CROCK-POT®** slow cooker. Cover; cook on LOW 8 hours.

2. Meanwhile, melt butter in large nonstick skillet over medium heat. Stir in apples and cinnamon; cook and stir 4 to 5 minutes or until tender. Stir in syrup; heat through.

3. Serve oatmeal with apple mixture and dried cranberries.

Makes 4 servings

Nutrition Information

Calories	179
Total Fat	6g
Saturated Fat	3g
Protein	19g
Carbohydrate	13g
Cholesterol	22mg
Fiber	1g
Sodium	704mg

Dietary Exchanges:
1 Starch, 2 Meat

Roasted Pepper and Sourdough Brunch Casserole

Nonstick cooking spray

3 **cups sourdough bread cubes**

1 **jar (12 ounces) roasted red pepper strips, drained and cut into strips**

1 **cup (4 ounces) shredded reduced-fat sharp Cheddar cheese**

1 **cup (4 ounces) shredded reduced-fat Monterey Jack cheese**

1 **cup fat-free cottage cheese**

1½ **cups cholesterol-free egg substitute**

1 **cup fat-free (skim) milk**

¼ **cup chopped fresh cilantro**

¼ **teaspoon black pepper**

1. Coat **CROCK-POT®** slow cooker with nonstick cooking spray. Add bread. Arrange roasted peppers evenly over bread cubes; sprinkle with Cheddar and Monterey Jack cheeses.

2. Place cottage cheese in food processor or blender; process until smooth. Add egg substitute and milk; process just until blended. Stir in cilantro and black pepper.

3. Pour egg and cheese mixture into **CROCK-POT®** slow cooker. Cover; cook on LOW 3 to 3½ hours or on HIGH 2 to 2½ hours or until eggs are firm but still moist.

Makes 8 servings

Banana Nut Bread

Note

Banana nut bread has always been a favorite way to use up those overripe bananas. Not only is it delicious, but it also freezes well for future use.

Tip

Recipe can be doubled for a 5-, 6- or 7-quart **CROCK-POT®** slow cooker.

⅓ **cup unsalted margarine or butter**

⅔ **cup sugar**

2 **eggs, well beaten**

2 **tablespoons dark corn syrup**

3 **medium ripe bananas, well mashed**

1¾ **cups all-purpose flour**

2 **teaspoons baking powder**

½ **teaspoon salt**

¼ **teaspoon baking soda**

⅓ **cup chopped walnuts**

1. Grease and flour inside of **CROCK-POT®** slow cooker. Cream butter in large bowl with electric mixer until fluffy. Slowly add sugar, eggs, corn syrup and mashed bananas. Beat until smooth.

2. Sift together flour, baking powder, salt and baking soda in small bowl. Slowly beat flour mixture into creamed mixture. Add walnuts and mix thoroughly. Pour into **CROCK-POT®** slow cooker. Cover; cook on HIGH 2 to 3 hours.

3. Let cool, then turn bread out onto serving platter.

Makes 8 servings

Nutrition Information

Calories	189
Total Fat	3g
Saturated Fat	1g
Protein	8g
Carbohydrate	33g
Cholesterol	71mg
Fiber	3g
Sodium	206mg

Dietary Exchanges:
½ Fruit, 1½ Starch, ½ Meat

Blueberry-Orange French Toast Casserole

Nonstick cooking spray

½ **cup sugar substitute***

½ **cup fat-free (skim) milk**

4 **egg whites**

2 **eggs**

1 **tablespoon grated orange peel**

½ **teaspoon vanilla**

6 **slices whole wheat bread, cut into 1-inch pieces**

1 **cup fresh (not frozen) blueberries**

Sugar-free maple syrup (optional)

*This recipe was tested with sucralose-based sugar substitute.

1. Coat **CROCK-POT®** slow cooker with nonstick cooking spray. Whisk sugar substitute and milk in medium bowl until dissolved. Whisk in egg whites, eggs, orange peel and vanilla. Add bread and blueberries; toss to coat.

2. Transfer egg mixture to **CROCK-POT®** slow cooker. Cover; cook on LOW 3 to 4 hours or on HIGH 1½ to 2 hours, or until tester inserted into center comes out mostly clean and dish is moist and tender.

3. Let stand 5 minutes before serving. Serve with syrup, if desired.

Makes 6 servings

Nutrition Information

Calories	60
Total Fat	0g
Saturated Fat	0g
Protein	<1g
Carbohydrate	15g
Cholesterol	0mg
Fiber	<1g
Sodium	6mg

Dietary Exchanges:
1 Fruit

Spiced Apple Tea

3 bags cinnamon herbal tea

3 cups boiling water

2 cups unsweetened apple juice

6 whole cloves

1 cinnamon stick

1. Place tea bags in **CROCK-POT®** slow cooker. Pour boiling water over tea bags; cover and let stand 10 minutes.

2. Remove and discard tea bags. Add apple juice, cloves and cinnamon stick to **CROCK-POT®** slow cooker. Cover; cook on LOW 2 to 3 hours.

3. Remove and discard cloves and cinnamon stick. Serve warm in mugs.

Makes 4 servings

Cherry-Orange Oatmeal

4 cups water

2 cups old-fashioned oats

4 tablespoons sugar substitute*

2 tablespoons unsweetened cocoa powder

2 cans (11 ounces) mandarin orange segments in light syrup, drained and rinsed

2 cups fresh pitted cherries or frozen dark sweet cherries

*This recipe was tested with sucralose-based sugar substitute.

1. Combine water, oats, sugar substitute and cocoa in **CROCK-POT®** slow cooker. Cover; cook on LOW 8 hours.

2. Serve oatmeal with oranges and cherries.

Makes 8 servings

Nutrition Information

Calories	150
Total Fat	2g
Saturated Fat	<1g
Protein	4g
Carbohydrate	39g
Cholesterol	0mg
Fiber	3g
Sodium	6mg

Dietary Exchanges:
1½ Fruit, 1 Starch

Nutrition Information

Calories	20
Total Fat	<1g
Saturated Fat	<1g
Protein	1g
Carbohydrate	3g
Cholesterol	3mg
Fiber	<1g
Sodium	16mg

Dietary Exchanges:
Free

Light Morning Mocha

- ¼ **cup sugar substitute**
- 2 **tablespoons unsweetened cocoa**
- 6 **cups brewed coffee**
- 1 **cup low-fat (1%) milk**
- 6 **tablespoons frozen low-fat whipped topping (optional)**

1. Combine sugar substitute and cocoa in **CROCK-POT®** slow cooker. Stir in coffee and milk. Cover; cook on LOW 3 hours or on HIGH 1½ hours or until hot. (May be kept warm on LOW up to 3 hours.)

2. Stir well before serving. Top with whipped topping, if desired.

Makes 8 servings

Spicy Apple Butter

5 **pounds tart cooking apples (McIntosh, Granny Smith, Rome Beauty or York Imperial), peeled, cored and quartered (about 10 large apples)**

1 **cup sugar**

½ **cup apple juice**

2 **teaspoons ground cinnamon**

½ **teaspoon ground cloves**

½ **teaspoon ground allspice**

1. Combine all ingredients in **CROCK-POT®** slow cooker. Cover; cook on LOW 8 to 10 hours or until apples are very tender.

2. Mash apples with potato masher. Cook, uncovered, 2 hours or until thickened, stirring occasionally to prevent sticking.

Makes about 6 cups

Nutrition Information

Calories	20
Total Fat	0g
Saturated Fat	0g
Protein	0g
Carbohydrate	5g
Cholesterol	0mg
Fiber	1g
Sodium	0mg

Dietary Exchanges:
Free

Serving Suggestion

Homemade apple butter is a great alternative to store-bought jam or jelly on your favorite toast or muffin.

Soups

Roast Tomato-Basil Soup

Nonstick cooking spray

2 cans (about 28 ounces each) peeled whole tomatoes, drained and 3 cups juice reserved

2½ tablespoons packed dark brown sugar

1 medium onion, finely chopped

3 cups fat-free reduced-sodium chicken broth

3 tablespoons tomato paste

¼ teaspoon ground allspice

1 can (5 ounces) evaporated milk

¼ cup shredded fresh basil (about 10 large leaves)

Salt and black pepper

1. Preheat oven to 450°F. Line baking sheet with foil; spray with nonstick cooking spray. Arrange tomatoes on foil in single layer. Sprinkle with brown sugar and top with onion. Bake 25 minutes or until tomatoes look dry and light brown. Let tomatoes cool slightly; finely chop.

2. Place tomato mixture, 3 cups reserved juice from tomatoes, broth, tomato paste and allspice in **CROCK-POT®** slow cooker. Mix well. Cover; cook on LOW 8 hours or on HIGH 4 hours.

3. Add evaporated milk and basil; season with salt and pepper. Turn **CROCK-POT®** slow cooker to HIGH; cook 30 minutes or until heated through.

Makes 8 servings

Nutrition Information

Calories	100
Total Fat	2g
Saturated Fat	1g
Protein	4g
Carbohydrate	17g
Cholesterol	5mg
Fiber	2g
Sodium	620mg

Dietary Exchanges:
2 Vegetable

Nutrition Information

Calories	250
Total Fat	12g
Saturated Fat	2g
Protein	11g
Carbohydrate	30g
Cholesterol	5mg
Fiber	12g
Sodium	750mg

Dietary Exchanges:
½ Vegetable, ½ Fruit,
1½ Starch, ½ Meat, 1½ Fat

Pumpkin Soup with Crumbled Bacon and Toasted Pumpkin Seeds

Nonstick cooking spray
2 **teaspoons olive oil**
½ **cup raw pumpkin seeds or pepitas**
2 **slices thick-cut bacon**
1 **medium onion, chopped**
1 **teaspoon kosher salt**
½ **teaspoon chipotle chili powder, or more to taste**
½ **teaspoon black pepper**
2 **cans (29 ounces each) 100% pumpkin purée**
4 **cups fat-free reduced-sodium chicken broth**
¾ **cup apple cider**
½ **cup fat-free half-and-half**
Sour cream (optional)

1. Coat **CROCK-POT®** slow cooker with nonstick cooking spray. Heat olive oil in small nonstick skillet over medium-high heat. Add pumpkin seeds; cook and stir until seeds begin to pop, about 1 minute. Spoon into small bowl and set aside.

2. Add bacon to skillet and cook until crisp. Remove bacon to paper towels and set aside to cool (do not drain drippings from pan). Crumble bacon. Reduce heat to medium and add onion to pan. Cook and stir 3 minutes or until onion is translucent. Stir in salt, chipotle chili powder and black pepper. Transfer to **CROCK-POT®** slow cooker.

3. Whisk pumpkin, broth and apple cider into **CROCK-POT®** slow cooker, whisking until smooth. Cover; cook on HIGH 4 hours.

4. Turn off **CROCK-POT®** slow cooker and remove lid. Whisk in half-and-half and adjust seasonings as necessary. Strain soup into bowls and garnish with pumpkin seeds, bacon and sour cream, if desired.

Makes 6 servings

Nutrition Information

Calories	280
Total Fat	5g
Saturated Fat	1g
Protein	10g
Carbohydrate	51g
Cholesterol	0mg
Fiber	6g
Sodium	520mg

Dietary Exchanges:
1½ Vegetable, 3 Starch, ½ Fat

Mediterranean Tomato, Oregano and Orzo Soup

- 2 tablespoons extra-virgin olive oil
- 1 large yellow onion, cut into wedges
- 3½ cups fresh tomatoes, peeled and crushed*
- 2 cups butternut squash, peeled and cut into ½-inch cubes
- 1 cup carrots, peeled and cut into matchstick pieces
- ½ cup zucchini, cleaned and sliced
- 1½ teaspoons minced fresh bay leaves or 3 whole dried bay leaves
- 1 tablespoon chopped fresh oregano
- 1 can (15 ounces) garbanzo beans, drained and rinsed
- 2 cups fat-free chicken broth
- 1 clove garlic, minced
- 1 teaspoon ground cumin
- ¾ teaspoon ground allspice
- ½ teaspoon salt
- ¼ teaspoon black pepper
- 1½ cups uncooked orzo pasta

To peel tomatoes, place one at a time in simmering water about 10 seconds. (Add 30 seconds if tomatoes are not fully ripened.) Immediately plunge into a bowl of cold water for another 10 seconds. Peel skin with a knife.

1. Heat oil in skillet over medium heat until hot. Add onion. Cook and stir until translucent and soft, about 10 minutes.

2. Add tomatoes, squash, carrots, zucchini, bay leaves and oregano to skillet. Cook and stir 25 to 30 minutes longer. Transfer to **CROCK-POT®** slow cooker.

3. Add remaining ingredients except orzo pasta. Cover; cook on LOW 7 to 8 hours or on HIGH 4 to 5 hours.

4. Turn **CROCK-POT®** slow cooker to HIGH. Add orzo. Cover; cook 30 to 45 minutes, or until pasta is done. Remove and discard dried bay leaves before serving, if used.

Makes 8 servings

Soups

Nutrition Information

Calories	240
Total Fat	7g
Saturated Fat	2g
Protein	18g
Carbohydrate	29g
Cholesterol	25mg
Fiber	7g
Sodium	670mg

Dietary Exchanges:
2½ Vegetable, 1 Starch,
1½ Meat, ½ Fat

Northwest Beef and Vegetable Soup

- 2 **tablespoons olive oil**
- 1 **pound lean stew beef, fat removed and cut into 1-inch cubes**
- 1 **medium onion, chopped**
- 1 **clove garlic, minced**
- 3½ **cups canned crushed tomatoes, undrained**
- 1 **can (about 15 ounces) no-salt-added white beans, drained and rinsed**
- 1 **pound buttercup squash, peeled and diced**
- 1 **medium turnip, peeled and diced**
- 1 **large potato, peeled and diced**
- 2 **medium stalks celery, sliced**
- 2 **tablespoons minced fresh basil**
- 1½ **teaspoons salt**
- 1 **teaspoon black pepper**
- 8 **cups water**

1. Heat oil in skillet over medium heat until hot. Sear beef on all sides, turning as it browns. Add onion and garlic during last few minutes of searing. Transfer to **CROCK-POT®** slow cooker.

2. Add remaining ingredients. Gently stir well to combine. Cover; cook on HIGH 2 hours. Turn **CROCK-POT®** slow cooker to LOW. Cook on LOW 4 to 6 hours longer, stirring occasionally and adjusting seasonings to taste.

Makes 8 servings

Nutrition Information

Calories	170
Total Fat	6g
Saturated Fat	3g
Protein	14g
Carbohydrate	15g
Cholesterol	45mg
Fiber	2g
Sodium	700mg

Dietary Exchanges:
½ Vegetable, ½ Starch,
1½ Meat, ½ Fat

Italian Sausage Soup

Sausage Meatballs

- 1 **pound bulk mild Italian sausage, casings removed**
- ½ **cup plain bread crumbs**
- ¼ **cup grated Parmesan cheese**
- ¼ **cup skim milk**
- 1 **egg**
- ½ **teaspoon dried basil**
- ½ **teaspoon black pepper**
- ¼ **teaspoon garlic salt**

Soup

- 4 **cups hot fat-free reduced-sodium chicken broth**
- 1 **tablespoon tomato paste**
- 2 **cloves garlic, minced**
- ¼ **teaspoon red pepper flakes**
- ½ **cup uncooked mini pasta shells***
- 1 **bag (10 ounces) baby spinach**

  Grated Parmesan cheese

*Or use other tiny pasta, such as ditalini (mini tubes) or farfallini (mini bowties).

1. Combine all meatball ingredients. Roll into marble-size balls.

2. Combine broth, tomato paste, garlic and red pepper flakes in **CROCK-POT®** slow cooker. Add meatballs. Cover; cook on LOW 5 to 6 hours.

3. Add pasta 30 minutes before serving. When pasta is tender, stir in spinach. Sprinkle with Parmesan cheese; serve immediately.

Makes 8 servings

Nutrition Information

Calories	135
Total Fat	4g
Saturated Fat	1g
Protein	8g
Carbohydrate	23g
Cholesterol	0mg
Fiber	5g
Sodium	242mg

Dietary Exchanges:
1½ Vegetable, 1 Starch,
½ Fat

Minestrone Alla Milanese

- 2 cans (about 14 ounces each) reduced-sodium beef broth
- 1 can (about 14 ounces) diced tomatoes
- 1 cup diced red potatoes
- 1 cup coarsely chopped carrots
- 1 cup coarsely chopped green cabbage
- 1 cup sliced zucchini
- ¾ cup chopped onion
- ¾ cup sliced fresh green beans
- ¾ cup coarsely chopped celery
- ¾ cup water
- 2 tablespoons olive oil
- 1 clove garlic, minced
- ½ teaspoon dried basil
- ¼ teaspoon dried rosemary
- 1 bay leaf
- 1 can (about 15 ounces) cannellini beans, rinsed and drained
  Grated Parmesan cheese (optional)

1. Combine all ingredients except cannellini beans and cheese in **CROCK-POT®** slow cooker; mix well. Cover; cook on LOW 5 to 6 hours.

2. Add cannellini beans. Cover; cook 1 hour or until vegetables are tender.

3. Remove and discard bay leaf before serving. Garnish with cheese, if desired.

Makes 8 to 10 servings

Nutrition Information

Calories	170
Total Fat	1g
Saturated Fat	0g
Protein	10g
Carbohydrate	28g
Cholesterol	0mg
Fiber	11g
Sodium	670mg

Dietary Exchanges:
1 Vegetable, 1½ Starch

French Lentil Rice Soup

6 cups fat-free reduced-sodium chicken broth or vegetable broth

1 cup lentils, picked over and rinsed

2 medium carrots, peeled and finely diced

1 small onion, finely chopped

2 medium stalks celery, finely diced

3 tablespoons uncooked white rice

2 tablespoons minced garlic

1 teaspoon herbes de Provence or dried thyme

½ teaspoon salt

⅛ teaspoon white pepper or black pepper

¼ cup heavy cream or sour cream, divided (optional)

¼ cup chopped parsley (optional)

1. Combine broth, lentils, carrots, onion, celery, rice, garlic, herbes de Provence, salt and pepper in **CROCK-POT®** slow cooker. Cover; cook on LOW 8 hours or on HIGH 4 to 5 hours.

2. Pureé soup, 1 cup at a time, in blender, returning blended soup to **CROCK-POT®** slow cooker after each batch.* (Or use immersion blender.)

3. Serve soup with cream and parsley, if desired.

Makes 6 servings

Use caution when processing hot liquids in blender. Vent lid of blender and cover with clean kitchen towel as directed by manufacturer.

Nutrition Information

Calories	210
Total Fat	9g
Saturated Fat	3g
Protein	14g
Carbohydrate	18g
Cholesterol	20mg
Fiber	2g
Sodium	750mg

Dietary Exchanges:
½ Vegetable, 1 Starch, 1 Fat

Note

To skin chicken easily, grasp skin with paper towel and pull away. Repeat with fresh paper towel for each piece of chicken, discarding skins and towels.

Creamy Farmhouse Chicken and Garden Soup

   Nonstick cooking spray
½ **package (16 ounces) frozen pepper stir-fry vegetable mix**
1 **cup frozen corn**
1 **medium zucchini, sliced**
2 **bone-in chicken thighs, skinned**
1 **can (about 14 ounces) fat-free chicken broth**
½ **teaspoon dried thyme**
½ **teaspoon minced garlic**
2 **ounces uncooked egg noodles**
1 **cup fat-free half-and-half**
½ **cup frozen green peas, thawed**
2 **tablespoons chopped parsley**
2 **tablespoons unsalted butter**
1 **teaspoon salt**
½ **teaspoon coarsely ground black pepper**

1. Coat **CROCK-POT®** slow cooker with nonstick cooking spray. Place stir-fry vegetables, corn and zucchini in bottom of **CROCK-POT®** slow cooker. Add chicken, broth, thyme and garlic. Cover; cook on HIGH 3 to 4 hours or until chicken is cooked through (165°F). Remove chicken and set aside to cool slightly.

2. Add noodles to **CROCK-POT®** slow cooker. Cover; cook 20 minutes or until noodles are tender.

3. Meanwhile, debone and chop chicken. Return to **CROCK-POT®** slow cooker. Stir in remaining ingredients. Let stand 5 minutes before serving.

Makes 6 servings

Nutrition Information

Calories	80
Total Fat	0g
Saturated Fat	0g
Protein	3g
Carbohydrate	16g
Cholesterol	0mg
Fiber	4g
Sodium	540mg

Dietary Exchanges:
1 Vegetable, ½ Starch

Rustic Vegetable Soup

1 **jar (16 ounces) picante sauce**

1 **package (10 ounces) frozen mixed vegetables, thawed**

1 **package (10 ounces) frozen cut green beans, thawed**

1 **can (about 10 ounces) condensed beef broth, undiluted**

1 **to 2 baking potatoes, cut into ½-inch pieces**

1 **medium green bell pepper, chopped**

½ **teaspoon sugar**

¼ **cup finely chopped fresh parsley**

Combine all ingredients except parsley in **CROCK-POT®** slow cooker. Cover; cook on LOW 8 hours or on HIGH 4 hours. Stir in parsley just before serving.

Makes 8 servings

Country Turkey and Veggie Soup

- **2 tablespoons unsalted butter, divided**
- **8 ounces sliced mushrooms**
- **½ cup chopped onion**
- **½ cup thinly sliced celery**
- **1 medium red bell pepper, chopped**
- **1 medium carrot, thinly sliced**
- **½ teaspoon dried thyme**
- **4 cups fat free reduced-sodium chicken or turkey broth**
- **4 ounces uncooked egg noodles**
- **2 cups chopped cooked skinless turkey breast**
- **1 cup fat-free half-and-half**
- **½ cup frozen peas, thawed**
- **¾ teaspoon salt**

1. Melt 1 tablespoon butter in large nonstick skillet over medium-high heat. Add mushrooms and onion; cook and stir 4 minutes or until onion is translucent.

2. Transfer mixture to **CROCK-POT®** slow cooker; add celery, bell pepper, carrot and thyme. Pour in broth. Cover; cook on HIGH 2½ hours.

3. Add noodles and turkey. Cover; cook 20 minutes. Stir in half-and-half, peas, remaining 1 tablespoon butter and salt. Cook until noodles are tender and soup is heated through.

Makes 8 servings

Nutrition Information

Calories	180
Total Fat	5g
Saturated Fat	3g
Protein	16g
Carbohydrate	18g
Cholesterol	45mg
Fiber	2g
Sodium	520mg

Dietary Exchanges:
½ Vegetable, ½ Starch, 1 Meat, ½ Fat

Nutrition Information

Calories	200
Total Fat	6g
Saturated Fat	2g
Protein	20g
Carbohydrate	22g
Cholesterol	60mg
Fiber	6g
Sodium	700mg

Dietary Exchanges:
1 Vegetable, 1 Starch

Mexican Chicken and Black Bean Soup

Nonstick cooking spray

4 **bone-in chicken thighs, skinned**

1 **cup finely chopped onion**

1 **can (about 14 ounces) fat-free reduced-sodium chicken broth**

1 **can (about 14 ounces) diced tomatoes with green chiles, undrained or diced tomatoes with Mexican seasoning**

1 **can (about 15 ounces) no-salt-added black beans, rinsed and drained**

1 **cup frozen corn**

1 **can (4 ounces) chopped mild green chiles**

1 **tablespoon chili powder**

1 **teaspoon ground cumin**

1 **teaspoon salt**

Optional toppings: sour cream, sliced avocado, shredded cheese, chopped cilantro, fried tortilla strips

1. Coat **CROCK-POT®** slow cooker with nonstick cooking spray. Add all ingredients except toppings. Cover; cook on HIGH 3 to 4 hours or until chicken is cooked through (165°F).

2. Remove chicken with slotted spoon; set aside to cool slightly. Debone and chop chicken. Return to **CROCK-POT®** slow cooker and stir well. Top as desired.

Makes 6 servings

Rich and Hearty Drumstick Soup

Nonstick cooking spray

2 **turkey drumsticks (about 1⅓ pounds total)**

2 **medium carrots, peeled and sliced**

1 **medium stalk celery, thinly sliced**

1 **cup chopped onion**

1 **teaspoon minced garlic**

½ **teaspoon poultry seasoning**

4½ **cups fat-free reduced-sodium chicken broth**

2 **ounces uncooked egg noodles**

¼ **cup chopped parsley**

1 **tablespoon unsalted butter**

¾ **teaspoon salt**

1. Coat **CROCK-POT®** slow cooker with nonstick cooking spray. Add drumsticks, carrots, celery, onion, garlic and poultry seasoning. Pour in broth. Cover; cook on HIGH 5 hours or until meat is falling off bones.

2. Remove drumsticks; set aside. Add noodles to **CROCK-POT®** slow cooker. Cover; cook 30 minutes or until noodles are tender. Meanwhile, debone turkey, remove skin and cut meat into bite-size pieces.

3. Stir turkey, parsley, butter and salt into **CROCK-POT®** slow cooker. Serve immediately.

Makes 6 servings

Nutrition Information	
Calories	190
Total Fat	5g
Saturated Fat	2g
Protein	23g
Carbohydrate	12g
Cholesterol	95mg
Fiber	2g
Sodium	720mg

Dietary Exchanges:
1 Vegetable, ½ Starch,
2½ Meat, ½ Fat

Soups

Nutrition Information

Calories.................................. 90
Total Fat................................3g
Saturated Fat........................1g
Protein 3g
Carbohydrate....................14g
Cholesterol..................100mg
Fiber..0g
Sodium.........................500mg

Dietary Exchanges:
½ Starch, ½ Fat

Note

Soup may be served hot or cold. To serve cold, allow soup to cool to room temperature. Cover and refrigerate up to 24 hours before serving.

Greek Lemon and Rice Soup

- **3 cans (about 14 ounces each) fat-free reduced-sodium chicken broth**
- **½ cup uncooked long grain white rice (not converted or instant rice)**
- **3 egg yolks**
- **¼ cup fresh lemon juice**
- **¼ teaspoon salt**
- **⅛ teaspoon white pepper or black pepper**
- **4 thin slices lemon (optional)**
- **4 teaspoons finely chopped parsley (optional)**

1. Combine broth and rice in **CROCK-POT®** slow cooker. Cover; cook on HIGH 2 to 3 hours or until rice is tender.

2. Turn **CROCK-POT®** slow cooker to LOW. Whisk egg yolks and lemon juice in medium bowl. Whisk large spoonful of hot rice mixture into egg yolk mixture. Whisk back into **CROCK-POT®** slow cooker. Cook 10 minutes.

3. Season with salt and pepper. Garnish with lemon slice and chopped parsley, if desired.

Makes 6 servings

Spring Pea and Mint Broth Soup

- **8 cups water**
- **3 medium carrots, cut into chunks**
- **2 medium onions, coarsely chopped**
- **3 leeks, coarsely chopped**
- **2 stalks celery, cut into chunks**
- **1 bunch fresh mint**
- **1 bag (32 ounces) frozen peas *or* 4 cups fresh spring peas**
- **1 tablespoon fresh lemon juice**
- **Kosher salt and black pepper**
- **Creme fraîche or sour cream**

1. Combine water, carrots, onions, leeks, celery and mint in **CROCK-POT®** slow cooker. Cover; cook on HIGH 5 hours.

2. Add peas and lemon juice. Cover; cook on LOW 4 to 5 hours or on HIGH 2 to 3 hours.

3. Season with salt and pepper. Ladle soup into bowls and garnish with dollop of creme fraîche.

Makes 6 to 8 servings

Nutrition Information

Calories	190
Total Fat	1g
Saturated Fat	0g
Protein	10g
Carbohydrate	36g
Cholesterol	0mg
Fiber	11g
Sodium	220mg

Dietary Exchanges:
2½ Vegetable, 1½ Starch

Note

Whether using frozen sweet peas or farmstand fresh spring peas, this soup is fun to make. The aroma of fresh mint that fills the house is reason enough to try it.

Nutrition Information

Calories................................. 90
Total Fat...............................0g
Saturated Fat.......................0g
Protein 4g
Carbohydrate....................21g
Cholesterol......................0mg
Fiber.......................................4g
Sodium......................... 750mg

Dietary Exchanges:
1½ Vegetable, ½ Starch

Easy Vegetarian Vegetable Bean Soup

- 3 **cans (about 14 ounces each) vegetable broth**
- 2 **cups cubed unpeeled potatoes**
- 2 **cups sliced leeks, white part only (about 3 medium)**
- 1 **can (about 14 ounces) diced tomatoes**
- 1 **medium onion, chopped**
- 1 **cup chopped or shredded cabbage**
- 1 **cup sliced celery**
- 1 **cup sliced carrots**
- 3 **cloves garlic, chopped**
- ⅛ **teaspoon dried rosemary**
- 1 **can (about 15 ounces) white beans, drained**
  Salt and black pepper

1. Combine broth, potatoes, leeks, tomatoes, onion, cabbage, celery, carrots, garlic and rosemary in **CROCK-POT®** slow cooker. Cover; cook on LOW 8 hours.

2. Stir in beans and season with salt and pepper. Cover; cook 30 minutes or until beans are heated through.

Makes 10 servings

Curried Sweet Potato and Carrot Soup

- **2 medium sweet potatoes, peeled and cut into ¾-inch pieces (about 5 cups)**
- **4 cups fat-free chicken broth**
- **2 cups baby carrots**
- **1 small onion, chopped**
- **¾ teaspoon curry powder**
- **½ teaspoon salt**
- **½ teaspoon black pepper, or to taste**
- **½ teaspoon ground cinnamon**
- **¼ teaspoon ground ginger**
- **¾ cup half-and-half**
- **1 tablespoon maple syrup**
- **Candied ginger (optional)**

1. Place sweet potatoes, broth, carrots, onion, curry powder, salt, pepper, cinnamon and ginger in **CROCK-POT®** slow cooker; mix well. Cover; cook on LOW 7 to 8 hours.

2. Purée soup, 1 cup at a time, in blender, returning blended soup to **CROCK-POT®** slow cooker after each batch. (Or use immersion blender.) Stir in half-and-half and maple syrup. Cover; cook on HIGH 15 minutes or until heated through. Garnish with strips of candied ginger.

Makes 8 servings

Nutrition Information

Calories	130
Total Fat	3g
Saturated Fat	2g
Protein	3g
Carbohydrate	24g
Cholesterol	10mg
Fiber	3g
Sodium	680mg

Dietary Exchanges:
½ Vegetable, 1 Starch, ½ Fat

Tip

For richer flavor, add a teaspoon of chicken soup base along with broth.

Nutrition Information

Calories.................................70
Total Fat..............................2g
Saturated Fat.......................1g
Protein 4g
Carbohydrate......................8g
Cholesterol....................5mg
Fiber.......................................2g
Sodium.........................800mg

Dietary Exchanges:
1 Vegetable

Cauliflower Soup

2 **heads cauliflower, cut into small florets**

8 **cups fat-free reduced-sodium chicken broth**

¾ **cup chopped celery**

¾ **cup chopped onion**

1 **teaspoon salt**

2 **teaspoons black pepper**

2 **cups whole milk or light cream**

1 **teaspoon reduced-sodium Worcestershire sauce**

1. Combine cauliflower, broth, celery, onions, salt and pepper in **CROCK-POT®** slow cooker. Cover; cook on LOW 7 to 8 hours or on HIGH 3 to 4 hours.

2. Using a hand mixer or hand blender, purée cooked ingredients until smooth. Mix in milk and Worcestershire sauce until smooth. Cook on HIGH 15 to 20 minutes longer before serving.

Makes 8 servings

Kale, Olive Oil and Parmesan Soup

- **2 tablespoons olive oil**
- **1 small Spanish onion, sliced**
- **3 cloves garlic, minced**
  Kosher salt and black pepper
- **2 pounds kale, washed and chopped**
- **8 cups fat-free reduced-sodium chicken stock**
  Parmesan cheese, grated
  Extra-virgin olive oil to garnish

1. Heat olive oil in large, heavy skillet over medium-high heat. Add onion and garlic; season with salt and pepper. Cook 4 to 5 minutes, stirring often, or until onion begins to soften. Stir in kale and cook, stirring, 2 to 4 minutes or until kale becomes bright green and tender. Remove from heat and reserve in refrigerator until needed.

2. Add chicken stock to **CROCK-POT®** slow cooker. Cover and cook on LOW 6 hours or on HIGH 3½ hours.

3. Add kale mixture and cook until heated through, 15 to 20 minutes.

4. Spoon soup into individual serving bowls, sprinkle with Parmesan and drizzle with extra-virgin olive oil immediately before serving.

Makes 6 servings

Nutrition Information	
Calories	140
Total Fat	6g
Saturated Fat	1g
Protein	7g
Carbohydrate	20g
Cholesterol	0mg
Fiber	4g
Sodium	670mg

Dietary Exchanges:
4 Vegetable, 1 Fat

Potato Leek Soup

1 package (32 ounces) fat-free reduced-sodium chicken broth

2 large baking potatoes (1½ to 2 pounds), peeled and cubed

3 large leeks, white and light green parts thinly sliced (about 2 cups)

¼ teaspoon white pepper

½ cup reduced-fat sour cream

Chopped fresh chives or dill (optional)

1. Combine broth, potatoes, leeks and pepper in **CROCK-POT®** slow cooker. Cover; cook on LOW 7 to 8 hours or on HIGH 3 to 4 hours or until vegetables are tender.

2. Pureé soup, 1 cup at a time, in blender, returning blended soup to **CROCK-POT®** slow cooker after each batch. (Or use immersion blender.) Stir in sour cream. Garnish with chives.

Makes 6 servings

Chicken and Vegetable Chowder

- **1 pound boneless, skinless chicken breasts, cut into 1-inch pieces**
- **1 can (about 14 ounces) reduced-sodium chicken broth**
- **1 can (about 10 ounces) condensed cream of potato soup, undiluted**
- **1 package (10 ounces) frozen broccoli florets, thawed**
- **1 cup sliced carrots**
- **1 jar (4½ ounces) sliced mushrooms, drained**
- **½ cup chopped onion**
- **½ cup whole kernel corn**
- **2 cloves garlic, minced**
- **½ teaspoon dried thyme**
- **⅓ cup half-and-half**

1. Combine chicken, broth, soup, broccoli, carrots, mushrooms, onion, corn, garlic and thyme in **CROCK-POT®** slow cooker; mix well. Cover; cook on LOW 5 to 6 hours.

2. Stir in half-and-half. Turn **CROCK-POT®** slow cooker to HIGH. Cover; cook 15 minutes or until heated through.

Makes 6 servings

Nutrition Information

Calories	188
Total Fat	5g
Saturated Fat	1g
Protein	22g
Carbohydrate	15g
Cholesterol	54mg
Fiber	2g
Sodium	704mg

Dietary Exchanges:
1 Starch, 2 Meat

Nutrition Information

Calories	200
Total Fat	7g
Saturated Fat	3g
Protein	11g
Carbohydrate	24g
Cholesterol	10mg
Fiber	6g
Sodium	750mg

Dietary Exchanges:
1 Vegetable, 1 Starch,
½ Meat, ½ Fat

Tip

Only small pasta varieties like tubetti, ditalini or small shell-shaped pasta should be used in this recipe. The low heat of a **CROCK-POT®** slow cooker won't allow larger pasta shapes to cook completely.

Pasta Fagioli Soup

- **2 cans (about 14 ounces each) fat-free reduced-sodium beef or vegetable broth**
- **1 can (about 15 ounces) Great Northern beans, rinsed and drained**
- **1 can (about 14 ounces) diced tomatoes**
- **2 medium zucchini, quartered lengthwise and sliced**
- **1 tablespoon olive oil**
- **1½ teaspoons minced garlic**
- **½ teaspoon dried basil**
- **½ teaspoon dried oregano**
- **½ cup uncooked ditalini, tubetti or small shell pasta**
- **½ cup garlic seasoned croutons**
- **½ cup shredded Asiago or Romano cheese**
- **3 tablespoons chopped fresh basil or Italian parsley (optional)**

1. Combine broth, beans, tomatoes, zucchini, oil, garlic, dried basil and oregano in **CROCK-POT®** slow cooker; mix well. Cover; cook on LOW 3 to 4 hours.

2. Stir in pasta. Cover; cook 1 hour or until pasta is tender.

3. Serve soup with croutons and cheese. Garnish with fresh basil.

Makes 6 servings

Roasted Corn and Red Pepper Chowder

- **2 tablespoons extra-virgin olive oil**
- **2 cups frozen corn, thawed or fresh corn kernels**
- **1 medium red bell pepper, cored, seeded and diced**
- **2 medium green onions, sliced**
- **4 cups fat-free reduced-sodium chicken broth**
- **2 baking potatoes, peeled and diced**
- **1 teaspoon salt**
- **½ teaspoon black pepper**
- **1 can (13 ounces) nonfat evaporated milk**
- **2 tablespoons minced flat-leaf parsley**

1. Heat oil in skillet over medium heat until hot. Add corn, bell pepper and onions. Cook and stir until vegetables are tender and lightly browned, about 7 to 8 minutes. Transfer to **CROCK-POT®** slow cooker.

2. Add broth, potatoes, salt and pepper. Stir well to combine. Cover; cook on LOW 7 to 9 hours or on HIGH 4 to 5 hours.

3. Thirty minutes before serving, add evaporated milk. Stir well to combine and continue cooking. To serve, garnish with parsley.

Makes 6 servings

Nutrition Information

Calories	200
Total Fat	5g
Saturated Fat	1g
Protein	8g
Carbohydrate	30g
Cholesterol	0mg
Fiber	4g
Sodium	790mg

Dietary Exchanges:
½ Vegetable, ½ Starch, 1 Fat, ½ Milk

Split Pea Soup With Turkey Ham

Nutrition Information

Calories	282
Total Fat	4g
Saturated Fat	1g
Protein	26g
Carbohydrate	39g
Cholesterol	28mg
Fiber	5g
Sodium	549mg

Dietary Exchanges:
2½ Starch, 2 Meat

- 4 cups no-salt-added chicken broth
- 1 cup raw green split peas
- 1 large carrot, peeled and diced
- 6 ounces turkey ham, cut into ½-inch pieces
- 1 small onion, diced
- 2 celery stalks, trimmed and diced
- 2 bay leaves
- 1 large clove garlic, minced
- ¼ teaspoon crushed dried thyme
- ⅛ teaspoon black pepper

Combine all ingredients in **CROCK-POT®** slow cooker. Cover; cook on LOW 6 hours. Remove and discard bay leaves before serving.

Makes 4 servings

Turkey-Tomato Soup

Nutrition Information

Calories	182
Total Fat	4g
Saturated Fat	1g
Protein	15g
Carbohydrate	25g
Cholesterol	27mg
Fiber	4g
Sodium	235mg

Dietary Exchanges:
1½ Starch, 1½ Meat

- 2 medium turkey thighs, boned, skinned and cut into 1-inch pieces
- 1¾ cups fat-free reduced-sodium chicken broth
- 1½ cups frozen corn
- 2 small white or red potatoes, cubed
- 1 cup chopped onion
- 1 can (8 ounces) no-salt-added tomato sauce
- 1 cup water
- ¼ cup tomato paste
- 2 tablespoons Dijon mustard
- 1 teaspoon hot pepper sauce
- ½ teaspoon sugar
- ½ teaspoon garlic powder
- ¼ cup finely chopped fresh parsley

Combine all ingredients except parsley in **CROCK-POT®** slow cooker. Cover; cook on LOW 9 to 10 hours. Stir in parsley just before serving.

Makes 6 servings

Simmering Hot and Sour Soup

- **2 cans (about 14 ounces each) fat-free reduced-sodium chicken broth**
- **1 cup chopped cooked chicken or pork**
- **4 ounces fresh shiitake mushroom caps, thinly sliced**
- **½ cup thinly sliced bamboo shoots**
- **3 tablespoons rice wine vinegar**
- **2 tablespoons low sodium soy sauce**
- **1½ teaspoons chili paste *or* 1 teaspoon hot chili oil**
- **4 ounces firm tofu, well drained and cut into ½-inch pieces**
- **2 teaspoons sesame oil**
- **2 tablespoons cornstarch**
- **2 tablespoons cold water**
- **Chopped cilantro or sliced green onions**

1. Combine broth, chicken, mushrooms, bamboo shoots, vinegar, soy sauce and chili paste in **CROCK-POT®** slow cooker. Cover; cook on LOW 3 to 4 hours or on HIGH 2 to 3 hours or until chicken is heated through (165°F).

2. Stir in tofu and sesame oil. Turn **CROCK-POT®** slow cooker to HIGH. Whisk cornstarch into water in small bowl; stir into soup. Cover; cook 10 minutes or until soup is thickened. Garnish with cilantro.

Makes 6 servings

Nutrition Information	
Calories	120
Total Fat	4g
Saturated Fat	0g
Protein	14g
Carbohydrate	8g
Cholesterol	30mg
Fiber	1g
Sodium	690mg

Dietary Exchanges:
½ Vegetable, 1 Meat, ½ Fat

Beef Main Dishes

Cajun Beef Stew

Nonstick cooking spray
1 tablespoon Cajun or blackened seasoning mix
1½ pounds beef stew meat, cut into 1½-inch pieces
2 medium red potatoes, cut into 1½-inch pieces
3 carrots, cut into 1-inch pieces
1 medium onion, cut into 1½-inch pieces
1 stalk celery, sliced
1 can (about 14 ounces) beef broth
3 tablespoons cornstarch
3 tablespoons water
Salt
1 cup frozen peas, thawed
¼ teaspoon dried thyme

1. Coat **CROCK-POT®** slow cooker with nonstick cooking spray. Sprinkle seasoning mix over meat in medium bowl; toss to coat. Place potatoes, carrots, onion and celery in **CROCK-POT®** slow cooker. Place beef on top of vegetables. Add broth. Cover; cook on LOW 7 to 8 hours or on HIGH 4 to 5 hours or until beef and vegetables are tender.

2. Transfer beef and vegetables to large bowl with slotted spoon. Cover and keep warm. Turn **CROCK-POT®** slow cooker to HIGH. Whisk cornstarch into water in small bowl until smooth; stir into **CROCK-POT®** slow cooker. Cover; cook 10 to 15 minutes or until thickened. Season with salt.

3. Return beef and vegetables to **CROCK-POT®** slow cooker. Stir in peas and thyme. Cook 15 minutes or until heated through.

Makes 4 servings

Nutrition Information

Calories	298
Total Fat	7g
Saturated Fat	2g
Protein	29g
Carbohydrate	29g
Cholesterol	55mg
Fiber	4g
Sodium	580mg

Dietary Exchanges:
2 Starch, 3 Meat

New England Chuck Roast

- 1 **lean beef chuck roast (3¼ pounds), string on**
- 2 **teaspoons salt**
- ¼ **teaspoon black pepper**
-   **Olive oil**
- 4 **cups water, divided**
- 2 **cups carrots, cut into 2-inch pieces**
- 2 **medium stalks celery, cut into 1-inch pieces**
- 1½ **cups yellow onion, cut into quarters**
- 4 **small red potatoes, cut into quarters**
- 3 **whole bay leaves**
- 2 **tablespoons white vinegar**
- 2 **tablespoons horseradish**
- 1 **head cabbage, cut into quarters or eighths**
- 4 **tablespoons all-purpose flour**
- 2 **tablespoons cornstarch**
-   **Salt and black pepper, to taste**

1. Season roast with salt and pepper. Heat oil in skillet over medium heat until hot. Sear roast on all sides, turning as it browns. Transfer to **CROCK-POT**® slow cooker.

2. Add 3 cups water, carrots, celery, onions, potatoes, bay leaves, vinegar and horseradish. Cover; cook on LOW 5 to 7 hours or on HIGH 2 to 4 hours.

3. One hour before serving add cabbage to **CROCK-POT**® slow cooker. Mix flour and cornstarch with 1 cup water. Add to **CROCK-POT**® slow cooker. Cover; cook on HIGH 1 hour, or until thickened. Season with salt and pepper, as desired. Remove and discard bay leaves before serving. Serve roast with sauce and vegetables.

Makes 12 servings

Nutrition Information

Calories	275
Total Fat	11g
Saturated Fat	3g
Protein	24g
Carbohydrate	20g
Cholesterol	73mg
Fiber	1g
Sodium	658mg

Dietary Exchanges:
1½ Starch, 3½ Meat

Texas-Style Barbecued Brisket

3 tablespoons Worcestershire sauce

2 cloves garlic, minced

1 tablespoon chili powder

1 teaspoon celery salt

1 teaspoon black pepper

1 teaspoon liquid smoke

1 beef brisket (3 to 4 pounds), trimmed of fat

2 bay leaves

Barbecue Sauce (page 69)

1. Combine Worcestershire sauce, garlic, chili powder, celery salt, pepper and liquid smoke in small bowl. Spread mixture on all sides of beef. Place beef in large resealable food storage bag; seal bag. Refrigerate 24 hours.

2. Place beef, marinade and bay leaves in **CROCK-POT®** slow cooker, cutting meat in half to fit, if necessary. Cover; cook on LOW 7 hours. Meanwhile, prepare Barbecue Sauce.

3. Remove and discard bay leaves. Remove beef from **CROCK-POT®** slow cooker and pour juices into 2-cup measure; let stand 5 minutes. Skim fat from juices. Stir 1 cup juices into Barbecue Sauce. Discard remaining juices.

4. Return beef and barbecue sauce mixture to **CROCK-POT®** slow cooker. Cover; cook 1 hour or until meat is fork-tender. Remove beef to cutting board. Cut across grain into ¼-inch-thick slices. Serve with sauce.

Makes 10 to 12 servings

Texas-Style
Barbecued Brisket

Barbecue Sauce

- **2 tablespoons vegetable oil**
- **1 onion, chopped**
- **2 cloves garlic, minced**
- **1 cup ketchup**
- **½ cup molasses**
- **¼ cup cider vinegar**
- **2 teaspoons chili powder**
- **½ teaspoon dry mustard**

1. Heat oil in medium saucepan over medium heat. Add onion and garlic; cook and stir until onion is tender.

2. Add remaining ingredients. Simmer over medium heat 5 minutes.

Makes about 1¾ cups sauce

Nutrition Information

Calories	40
Total Fat	1g
Saturated Fat	0g
Protein	0g
Carbohydrate	7g
Cholesterol	0mg
Fiber	0g
Sodium	135mg

Dietary Exchanges:
½ Other

Nutrition Information

Calories	220
Total Fat	5g
Saturated Fat	2g
Protein	28g
Carbohydrate	13g
Cholesterol	50mg
Fiber	2g
Sodium	210mg

Dietary Exchanges:
1 Vegetable, 3½ Meat

Horseradish Roast Beef and Potatoes

- **1 tablespoon freshly grated horseradish**
- **1 tablespoon Dijon mustard**
- **1 tablespoon minced fresh parsley**
- **1 teaspoon thyme, basil or oregano**
- **3 pounds lean beef roast**
- **1 to 2 pounds Yukon Gold potatoes, peeled and quartered**
- **1 pound mushrooms, cut into large chunks**
- **2 cans (about 10 ounces each) fat-free reduced-sodium beef broth**
- **2 large tomatoes, seeded and diced**
- **1 large onion, sliced**
- **1 green bell pepper, chopped**
- **1 red bell pepper, chopped**
- **1 cup red wine**
- **3 cloves garlic, minced**
- **1 bay leaf**
- **Salt and pepper**

1. Combine horseradish, mustard, parsley and thyme in small bowl. Place roast in **CROCK-POT®** slow cooker and spread paste over roast.

2. Add remaining ingredients to **CROCK-POT®** slow cooker and season with salt and pepper. Add enough water to cover roast and vegetables. Cover; cook on HIGH 2 hours. Turn **CROCK-POT®** slow cooker to LOW; cook 4 to 6 hours or until roast and vegetables are tender. Remove and discard bay leaf before serving.

Makes 12 servings

Nutrition Information

Calories	260
Total Fat	11g
Saturated Fat	3g
Protein	29g
Carbohydrate	10g
Cholesterol	65mg
Fiber	2g
Sodium	350mg

Dietary Exchanges:
1½ Vegetable, ½ Fat,
4 Meat

Merlot'd Beef and Sun-Dried Tomato Portobello Ragout

- 1 jar (7 ounces) sun-dried tomatoes packed in oil, drained, with 3 tablespoons oil reserved
- 1 lean boneless chuck roast (about 2¾ pounds), cut into 1½-inch pieces
- 1 can (about 10 ounces) fat-free reduced-sodium beef broth
- 6 ounces sliced portobello mushrooms
- 1 medium green bell pepper, cut into thin strips
- 1 medium orange or yellow bell pepper, cut into thin strips
- 1 medium onion, cut into 8 wedges
- 2 teaspoons dried oregano
- ½ teaspoon salt
- ¼ teaspoon garlic powder
- ½ cup Merlot or other red wine
- 2 tablespoons Worcestershire sauce
- 1 tablespoon balsamic vinegar
- 1 tablespoon cornstarch
  Salt and black pepper, to taste
  Mashed potatoes, rice or egg noodles

1. Heat 1 tablespoon reserved oil from sun-dried tomatoes in large nonstick skillet over medium-high heat. Add one third of beef and brown on all sides. Transfer to **CROCK-POT®** slow cooker. Repeat with remaining oil and beef.

2. Add broth to skillet; stirring to scrape up browned bits. Pour mixture over beef. Add sun-dried tomatoes, mushrooms, bell peppers, onion, oregano, salt and garlic powder to **CROCK-POT®** slow cooker; mix well.

3. Combine Merlot and Worcestershire sauce in small bowl; reserve ¼ cup. Gently stir remaining Merlot mixture into **CROCK-POT®** slow cooker. Cover; cook on LOW 8 to 9 hours or on HIGH 4 to 5 hours or until beef is tender.

4. Turn **CROCK-POT®** slow cooker to HIGH. Stir vinegar and cornstarch into reserved ¼ cup Merlot mixture until cornstarch is dissolved. Add to **CROCK-POT®** slow cooker; stir until well blended. Cover; cook 15 minutes or until thickened slightly. Add salt and pepper, if desired. Serve with mashed potatoes.

Makes 10 servings

Nutrition Information

Calories	278
Total Fat	5g
Saturated Fat	2g
Protein	22g
Carbohydrate	34g
Cholesterol	38mg
Fiber	3g
Sodium	295mg

Dietary Exchanges:
2 Starch, 2 Meat

Greek-Style Meatballs and Spinach

- ½ **cup old-fashioned oats**
- ¼ **cup minced onion**
- 1 **clove garlic, minced**
- ¼ **teaspoon crushed dried oregano**
- ⅛ **teaspoon black pepper**
- ¼ **cup cholesterol-free egg substitute**
- 8 **ounces lean ground lamb**
- 1 **cup no-salt-added beef broth**
- ¼ **teaspoon salt**
- ½ **cup fat-free plain yogurt**
- 1 **teaspoon all-purpose flour**
- 4 **cups fresh baby spinach, coarsely chopped**
- 1⅓ **cups cooked no-yolk egg noodles**

1. Combine oats, onion, garlic, oregano and pepper in medium bowl. Stir in egg substitute. Add ground lamb; mix well but do not knead. Shape lamb mixture into 16 balls. Place in **CROCK-POT®** slow cooker. Add broth and salt. Cover; cook on LOW 6 hours.

2. Stir yogurt and flour in small bowl. Spoon about ¼ cup cooking liquid from **CROCK-POT®** slow cooker into yogurt. Stir until smooth. Stir yogurt mixture into **CROCK-POT®** slow cooker. Add spinach. Cover; cook 10 minutes or until heated through. Serve over noodles.

Makes 4 servings

Nutrition Information

Calories	296
Total Fat	8g
Saturated Fat	3g
Protein	28g
Carbohydrate	25g
Cholesterol	57mg
Fiber	4g
Sodium	381mg

Dietary Exchanges:
3 Vegetable, ½ Fruit,
½ Starch, 3 Meat

Sauerbraten

- **1 boneless beef rump roast (1¼ pounds)**
- **3 cups baby carrots**
- **1½ cups fresh or frozen pearl onions**
- **¼ cup raisins**
- **½ cup water**
- **½ cup red wine vinegar**
- **1 tablespoon honey**
- **½ teaspoon salt**
- **½ teaspoon dry mustard**
- **½ teaspoon garlic-pepper seasoning**
- **¼ teaspoon ground cloves**
- **¼ cup crushed crisp gingersnap cookies (5 cookies)**

1. Heat large nonstick skillet over medium-high heat; brown roast on all sides. Place roast, carrots, onions and raisins in **CROCK-POT®** slow cooker .

2. Combine water, vinegar, honey, salt, mustard, garlic-pepper seasoning and cloves in large bowl; mix well. Pour mixture over meat and vegetables in **CROCK-POT®** slow cooker. Cover; cook on LOW 4 to 6 hours.

3. Transfer roast to cutting board; cover with foil. Let stand 10 to 15 minutes before slicing. Remove vegetables from **CROCK-POT®** slow cooker with slotted spoon to bowl; cover and keep warm.

4. Turn **CROCK-POT®** slow cooker to HIGH. Stir crushed cookies into **CROCK-POT®** slow cooker. Cover; cook 10 to 15 minutes or until sauce is thickened. Serve meat and vegetables with sauce.

Makes 5 servings

Nutrition Information

Calories	210
Total Fat	8g
Saturated Fat	3g
Protein	29g
Carbohydrate	6g
Cholesterol	65mg
Fiber	1g
Sodium	740mg

Dietary Exchanges:
1 Vegetable, 4 Meat

Tip

Cooking times are guidelines. **CROCK-POT®** slow cookers, just like ovens, cook differently depending on a variety of factors. For example, cooking times will be longer at higher altitudes. You may need to slightly adjust cooking times for your **CROCK-POT®** slow cooker.

Slow Cooker Pepper Steak

2 tablespoons vegetable oil

2¾ pounds lean boneless beef top sirloin steak, cut into strips

1 tablespoon (5 to 6 cloves) minced garlic

1 medium onion, chopped

½ cup reduced-sodium soy sauce

2 teaspoons sugar

1 teaspoon salt

½ teaspoon ground ginger

½ teaspoon black pepper

3 green bell peppers, cut into strips

¼ cup cold water

1 tablespoon cornstarch

Hot cooked white rice

1. Heat oil in large nonstick skillet over medium-low heat; brown steak strips in 2 batches. Add garlic to skillet; cook and stir 2 minutes. Transfer steak and garlic to **CROCK-POT®** slow cooker.

2. Add onion, soy sauce, sugar, salt, ginger and black pepper to **CROCK-POT®** slow cooker; mix well. Cover; cook on LOW 6 to 8 hours or until meat is tender. Add bell pepper strips during final hour of cooking.

3. Turn **CROCK-POT®** slow cooker to HIGH. Whisk water into cornstarch in small bowl until smooth; stir into **CROCK-POT®** slow cooker. Cook, uncovered, 15 minutes or until thickened. Serve with rice.

Makes 10 servings

Nutrition Information

Calories	43
Total Fat	2g
Saturated Fat	<1g
Protein	3g
Carbohydrate	4g
Cholesterol	11mg
Fiber	<1g
Sodium	15mg

Dietary Exchanges:
1 Vegetable, ½ Fat

Stuffed Baby Bell Peppers

1 tablespoon extra-virgin olive oil

½ medium onion, chopped

½ pound ground beef, chicken or turkey

½ cup cooked white rice

1 tablespoon dried dill weed

3 tablespoons chopped fresh parsley

2 tablespoons lemon juice

1 tablespoon tomato paste, divided

½ teaspoon salt

⅛ teaspoon black pepper

1 bag yellow and red baby bell peppers
(about 2 dozen baby bell peppers)

¼ cup vegetable, chicken or beef broth

1. Heat oil in medium nonstick skillet over medium heat. Add onion; cook and stir until transluscent. Add ground beef; cook until cooked through and lightly browned, stirring to break up meat. Drain fat. Transfer to large bowl.

2. Add rice, dill weed, parsley, lemon juice, 1½ teaspoons tomato paste, salt and black pepper; stir until well combined. Set aside.

3. Cut small slit in the side of each baby bell pepper and run under cold water to wash out seeds. Fill each pepper with 2 to 3 teaspoons seasoned beef. Place peppers in **CROCK-POT®** slow cooker, slit side up. Add broth and remaining 1½ teaspoons tomato paste. Cover; cook on LOW 5 hours or on HIGH 2½ hours.

Makes 16 to 18 servings

Nutrition Information

Calories	190
Total Fat	7g
Saturated Fat	3g
Protein	23g
Carbohydrate	7g
Cholesterol	80mg
Fiber	1g
Sodium	380mg

Dietary Exchanges:
½ Vegetable, 2½ Meat

That's Italian Meat Loaf

- **1 can (8 ounces) tomato sauce, divided**
- **1 egg, lightly beaten**
- **½ cup chopped onion**
- **½ cup chopped green bell pepper**
- **⅓ cup seasoned dry bread crumbs**
- **2 tablespoons grated Parmesan cheese**
- **½ teaspoon garlic powder**
- **¼ teaspoon black pepper**
- **1 pound ground beef**
- **½ pound ground pork**
- **1 cup (4 ounces) shredded Asiago cheese**

1. Reserve ⅓ cup tomato sauce; refrigerate. Combine remaining tomato sauce and egg in large bowl. Stir in onion, bell pepper, bread crumbs, Parmesan cheese, garlic powder and black pepper. Add beef and pork; mix well and shape into loaf.

2. Carefully transfer meat loaf to **CROCK-POT®** slow cooker. Cover; cook on LOW 8 to 10 hours or on HIGH 4 to 6 hours.

3. Spread meat loaf with reserved tomato sauce; sprinkle with Asiago cheese. Cover; cook 15 minutes or until cheese is melted.

Makes 8 servings

Barbecued Meatballs

2	**pounds (32 ounces) 95% lean ground beef**
1⅓	**cups ketchup, divided**
3	**tablespoons seasoned dry bread crumbs**
1	**egg, lightly beaten**
2	**tablespoons dried onion flakes**
¾	**teaspoon garlic salt**
½	**teaspoon black pepper**
1	**cup packed light brown sugar**
1	**can (6 ounces) tomato paste**
¼	**cup reduced-sodium soy sauce**
¼	**cup cider vinegar**
1½	**teaspoons hot pepper sauce**

1. Preheat oven to 350°F. Combine beef, ⅓ cup ketchup, bread crumbs, egg, onion flakes, garlic salt and black pepper in medium bowl. Mix lightly but thoroughly; shape into 1-inch meatballs.

2. Place meatballs in 2 (15×10-inch) jelly-roll pans or shallow roasting pans. Bake 18 minutes or until browned. Transfer to **CROCK-POT®** slow cooker.

3. Mix remaining 1 cup ketchup, brown sugar, tomato paste, soy sauce, vinegar and hot pepper sauce in medium bowl; pour over meatballs. Cover; cook on LOW 4 hours.

Makes about 4 dozen meatballs

Nutrition Information

Calories	139
Total Fat	5g
Saturated Fat	2g
Protein	8g
Carbohydrate	16g
Cholesterol	32mg
Fiber	<1g
Sodium	441mg

Dietary Exchanges:
1 Starch, 1 Meat, ½ Fat

Variation

Barbecued Franks: Arrange 2 (12-ounce) packages or 3 (8-ounce) packages cocktail franks in slow cooker. Combine 1 cup ketchup with brown sugar, tomato paste, soy sauce, vinegar and hot pepper sauce in medium bowl; pour over franks. Cook according to directions for Barbecued Meatballs.

Nutrition Information

Calories.............................289
Total Fat...............................5g
Saturated Fat......................2g
Protein................................22g
Carbohydrate....................39g
Cholesterol.....................67mg
Fiber.....................................6g
Sodium...........................772mg

Dietary Exchanges:
2 Vegetable, 2 Starch,
2 Meat

Hungarian Lamb Goulash

> 1 **package (16 ounces) frozen cut green beans, thawed**
> 1 **cup chopped onion**
> 1¼ **pounds lean lamb for stew, cut into 1-inch cubes**
> 1 **can (about 15 ounces) chunky tomato sauce**
> 1¾ **cups fat-free reduced-sodium chicken broth**
> 1 **can (6 ounces) tomato paste**
> 4 **teaspoons paprika**
> 3 **cups hot cooked egg noodles**

1. Place green beans and onion in **CROCK-POT®** slow cooker. Top with lamb.

2. Combine tomato sauce, broth, tomato paste and paprika in large bowl; mix well. Pour over lamb mixture. Cover; cook on LOW 6 to 8 hours. Stir goulash before serving over noodles.

Makes 6 servings

Beef with Apples and Sweet Potatoes

- **1 lean boneless beef chuck shoulder roast (about 2 pounds)**
- **1 can (40 ounces) sweet potatoes, drained**
- **2 medium apples, cored and sliced**
- **2 small onions, sliced**
- **½ cup fat-free reduced-sodium beef broth**
- **2 cloves garlic, minced**
- **1 teaspoon salt**
- **1 teaspoon dried thyme, divided**
- **¾ teaspoon black pepper, divided**
- **2 tablespoons cold water**
- **1 tablespoon cornstarch**
- **¼ teaspoon ground cinnamon**

1. Trim excess fat from beef and discard. Cut beef into 2-inch pieces. Place beef, sweet potatoes, apples, onions, broth, garlic, salt, ½ teaspoon thyme and ½ teaspoon pepper in **CROCK-POT®** slow cooker. Cover; cook on LOW 8 to 9 hours.

2. Transfer beef, sweet potatoes and apples to platter; cover with foil to keep warm. Let cooking liquid stand 5 minutes to allow fat to rise; skim off fat and discard.

3. Whisk water, cornstarch, remaining ½ teaspoon thyme, ¼ teaspoon pepper and cinnamon in small bowl until smooth; stir into cooking liquid. Turn **CROCK-POT®** slow cooker to HIGH. Cook 15 minutes or until cooking liquid is thickened. Serve sauce over beef, sweet potatoes and apples.

Makes 8 servings

Nutrition Information

Calories	330
Total Fat	7g
Saturated Fat	2g
Protein	27g
Carbohydrate	39g
Cholesterol	65mg
Fiber	4g
Sodium	460mg

Dietary Exchanges:
½ Vegetable, ½ Fruit, 1½ Starch, 3½ Meat

Tip

Because **CROCK-POT®** slow cookers cook at a low heat for a long time, they're a great way to cook dishes calling for less tender cuts of meat, since long, slow cooking helps tenderize these cuts.

Nutrition Information

Calories	212
Total Fat	8g
Saturated Fat	3g
Protein	15g
Carbohydrate	17g
Cholesterol	32mg
Fiber	6g
Sodium	290mg

Dietary Exchanges:
1 Starch, 1½ Meat, 1 Fat

Chili Mac

- 1 **pound ground beef or turkey**
- ½ **cup chopped onion**
- 1 **can (about 14 ounces) diced tomatoes, drained**
- 1 **can (8 ounces) tomato sauce**
- 2 **tablespoons chili powder**
- 1 **teaspoon garlic salt**
- ½ **teaspoon ground cumin**
- ¼ **teaspoon red pepper flakes**
- ¼ **teaspoon black pepper**
- 8 **ounces uncooked elbow macaroni**
  Shredded Cheddar cheese (optional)

1. Heat large nonstick skillet over medium heat; brown beef and onion 6 to 8 minutes, stirring to break up meat. Drain fat. Transfer beef mixture to **CROCK-POT®** slow cooker.

2. Add tomatoes, tomato sauce, chili powder, garlic salt, cumin, red pepper flakes and black pepper; mix well. Cover; cook on LOW 4 hours.

3. Cook macaroni according to package directions. Add macaroni to **CROCK-POT®** slow cooker; mix well. Cover; cook 1 hour. Top with cheese, if desired.

Makes 4 to 6 servings

Niku Jaga (Japanese Beef Stew)

- **2 tablespoons vegetable oil**
- **2 pounds beef stew meat, cut in 1-inch cubes**
- **4 medium carrots, peeled and diagonally sliced**
- **3 medium Yukon Gold potatoes, peeled and chopped**
- **1 medium white onion, peeled and chopped**
- **1 cup water**
- **½ cup Japanese sake or dry white wine**
- **¼ cup sugar**
- **¼ cup reduced-sodium soy sauce**
- **1 teaspoon salt**

1. Heat oil in skillet over medium heat until hot. Sear beef on all sides, turning as it browns. Transfer beef to **CROCK-POT®** slow cooker.

2. Add remaining ingredients. Stir well to combine. Cover; cook on LOW 10 to 12 hours or on HIGH 4 to 6 hours.

Makes 10 servings

Nutrition Information

Calories	230
Total Fat	8g
Saturated Fat	3g
Protein	22g
Carbohydrate	16g
Cholesterol	50mg
Fiber	2g
Sodium	510mg

Dietary Exchanges:
½ Vegetable, 3 Meat, ½ Fat

Nutrition Information

Calories	278
Total Fat	9g
Saturated Fat	3g
Protein	29g
Carbohydrate	19g
Cholesterol	60mg
Fiber	3g
Sodium	116mg

Dietary Exchanges:
1 Starch, 4 Meat

Beef Stew with Bacon, Onion and Sweet Potatoes

Nonstick cooking spray
1 pound beef stew meat, cut into 1-inch chunks
1 can (about 14 ounces) beef broth
2 medium sweet potatoes, peeled and cut into 2-inch chunks
1 large onion, cut into 1½-inch chunks
2 slices thick-cut bacon, diced
1 teaspoon dried thyme
1 teaspoon salt
¼ teaspoon black pepper
2 tablespoons cornstarch
2 tablespoons water

1. Coat **CROCK-POT®** slow cooker with nonstick cooking spray. Combine all ingredients except cornstarch and water in **CROCK-POT®** slow cooker; mix well. Cover; cook on LOW 7 to 8 hours or on HIGH 4 to 5 hours or until meat and vegetables are tender.

2. Transfer beef and vegetables to serving bowl with slotted spoon; cover with foil to keep warm.

3. Turn **CROCK-POT®** slow cooker to HIGH. Whisk cornstarch into water in small bowl; stir into cooking liquid. Cover; cook 15 minutes or until thickened. To serve, spoon sauce over beef and vegetables.

Makes 4 servings

Tavern Burger

- **2 pounds 95% lean ground beef**
- ½ **cup ketchup**
- ¼ **cup packed brown sugar**
- ¼ **cup prepared yellow mustard**
- **Hamburger buns**

1. Heat medium nonstick skillet over medium-high heat; brown beef 6 to 8 minutes, stirring to break up meat. Drain fat. Transfer to **CROCK-POT®** slow cooker.

2. Add ketchup, sugar and mustard to **CROCK-POT®** slow cooker; mix well. Cover; cook on LOW 4 to 6 hours. Serve on buns.

Makes 8 servings

Nutrition Information

Calories	200
Total Fat	6g
Saturated Fat	3g
Protein	25g
Carbohydrate	11g
Cholesterol	70mg
Fiber	0g
Sodium	330mg

Dietary Exchanges:
3½ Meat, ½ Other

Tip

This is also known to some people as "BBQs" or "loose-meat sandwiches."

Nutrition Information

Calories	200
Total Fat	6g
Saturated Fat	3g
Protein	28g
Carbohydrate	5g
Cholesterol	65mg
Fiber	1g
Sodium	350mg

Dietary Exchanges:
1 Vegetable, 4 Meat

Dilly Beef Sandwiches

1 **lean boneless beef chuck roast (2¾ pounds)**

1 **jar (6 ounces) sliced dill pickles**

1 **can (about 14 ounces) crushed tomatoes with Italian seasoning**

1 **medium onion, diced**

4 **cloves garlic, minced**

1 **teaspoon mustard seeds**

Hamburger buns, toasted

Optional toppings: lettuce, sliced tomatoes, sliced red onions

1. Trim excess fat from beef and discard. Cut beef into chunks. Place in **CROCK-POT®** slow cooker. Pour pickles with juice over beef. Add tomatoes, onion, garlic and mustard seeds. Cover; cook on LOW 8 to 10 hours.

2. Remove beef from **CROCK-POT®** slow cooker; shred with two forks. Return beef to tomato mixture; stir to coat. Serve on buns with desired toppings.

Makes 10 servings

Lamb and Vegetable Stew

- **2 cups sliced mushrooms**
- **1 large red bell pepper, diced**
- **1 large carrot, cut into ½-inch-thick slices**
- **1 small unpeeled new potato, diced**
- **1 small parsnip, cut into ½-inch-thick slices**
- **1 large leek, white part only, chopped**
- **1 clove garlic, minced**
- **½ cup reduced-sodium chicken broth**
- **½ teaspoon dried thyme**
- **¼ teaspoon dried rosemary**
- **⅛ teaspoon black pepper**
- **12 ounces lamb shoulder meat, cut into 1-inch pieces**
- **2 tablespoons all-purpose flour**
- **½ teaspoon salt (optional)**

1. Place mushrooms, bell pepper, carrot, potato, parsnip, leek and garlic in **CROCK-POT®** slow cooker. Add broth, thyme, rosemary and black pepper; stir. Add lamb. Cover; cook on LOW 6 to 7 hours.

2. Whisk flour into 2 tablespoons cooking liquid from **CROCK-POT®** slow cooker in small bowl. Stir flour mixture into **CROCK-POT®** slow cooker. Cover; cook 10 minutes. Stir in salt, if desired.

Makes 4 servings

Nutrition Information

Calories	204
Total Fat	4g
Saturated Fat	1g
Protein	21g
Carbohydrate	55g
Cholesterol	82mg
Fiber	3g
Sodium	82mg

Dietary Exchanges:
1 Vegetable, 1 Starch, 2 Meat

Kick'n Chili

- **2 pounds (32 ounces) 95% lean ground beef**
- **1 tablespoon *each* cumin, chili powder, paprika, dried oregano and black pepper**
- **2 cloves garlic, minced**
- **2 teaspoons red pepper flakes**
- **1½ teaspoons salt**
- **¼ teaspoon ground red pepper**
- **1 tablespoon vegetable oil**
- **3 cans (about 10 ounces each) diced tomatoes with green chiles**
- **1 jar (16 ounces) salsa**
- **1 medium onion, chopped**

1. Combine beef, cumin, chili powder, paprika, oregano, black pepper, garlic, red pepper flakes, salt and ground red pepper in large bowl.

2. Heat oil in large nonstick skillet over medium-high heat; brown beef mixture 6 to 8 minutes, stirring to separate meat. Drain fat. Add tomatoes, salsa and onion; mix well. Transfer mixture to **CROCK-POT®** slow cooker. Cover; cook on LOW 4 to 6 hours.

Makes 8 servings

Shredded Beef Wraps

1 **lean beef flank steak or beef skirt steak (1 to 1½ pounds)**

1 **cup fat-free reduced-sodium beef broth**

½ **cup sun-dried tomatoes (not packed in oil), chopped**

3 **to 4 cloves garlic, minced**

¼ **teaspoon ground cumin**

4 **flour tortillas, warmed**

Toppings: shredded lettuce, diced tomatoes and shredded Monterey Jack cheese

1. Cut steak into quarters. Place steak, broth, sun-dried tomatoes, garlic and cumin in **CROCK-POT®** slow cooker. Cover; cook on LOW 7 to 8 hours or until meat is very tender.

2. Remove beef from slow cooker; shred beef with two forks or cut into thin strips. Place remaining juices from **CROCK-POT®** slow cooker in blender or food processor; blend until smooth.

3. Spoon beef onto tortillas with small amount of sauce. Add desired toppings. Roll up and serve.

Makes 4 servings

Nutrition Information

Calories	280
Total Fat	9g
Saturated Fat	3g
Protein	28g
Carbohydrate	21g
Cholesterol	35mg
Fiber	1g
Sodium	540mg

Dietary Exchanges:
1 Vegetable, 1 Starch, 3½ Meat

Beef and Parsnip Stroganoff

1	**cube beef bouillon**
¾	**cup boiling water**
1	**boneless beef top round steak (about ¾ pound), trimmed**
	Nonstick cooking spray
2	**cups cubed peeled parsnips or potatoes**
1	**medium onion, halved and thinly sliced**
¾	**pound mushrooms, sliced**
2	**teaspoons minced garlic**
¼	**teaspoon black pepper**
1	**tablespoon plus 1½ teaspoons all-purpose flour**
¼	**cup water**
4	**ounces uncooked yolk-free wide noodles**
3	**tablespoons reduced-fat sour cream**
1½	**teaspoons Dijon mustard**
¼	**teaspoon cornstarch**
1	**tablespoon chopped parsley**

Nutrition Information

Calories	347
Total Fat	6g
Saturated Fat	2g
Protein	28g
Carbohydrate	46g
Cholesterol	46mg
Fiber	5g
Sodium	242mg

Dietary Exchanges:
3 Starch, 2 Meat

1. Dissolve bouillon in ¾ cup boiling water; cool. Meanwhile, cut steak lengthwise in half, then crosswise into ½-inch strips. Spray large nonstick skillet with nonstick cooking spray; heat over high heat. Add beef; cook and stir about 4 minutes or until beef begins to brown. Transfer beef and juices to **CROCK-POT®** slow cooker.

2. Spray skillet with nonstick cooking spray. Add parsnips and onion; cook and stir about 4 minutes or until browned. Add mushrooms, garlic and pepper; cook and stir about 5 minutes or until mushrooms are tender. Transfer mixture to **CROCK-POT®** slow cooker.

3. Whisk flour into ¼ cup water in small bowl until smooth. Combine flour mixture and bouillon in **CROCK-POT®** slow cooker; stir until blended. Cover; cook on LOW 4½ to 5 hours or until beef and parsnips are tender.

4. Prepare noodles according to package directions. Remove beef and vegetables from **CROCK-POT®** slow cooker with slotted spoon to large bowl, reserving cooking liquid. Blend sour cream, mustard and cornstarch in medium bowl. Gradually add reserved cooking liquid to sour cream mixture; stir well to blend. Stir sour cream mixture into beef and vegetable mixture. Serve over hot noodles. Sprinkle with parsley.

Makes 4 servings

Slow Cooker Steak Fajitas

- **1 lean beef flank steak (about 1 pound)**
- **1 medium onion, cut into strips**
- **½ cup medium salsa, plus additional for garnish**
- **2 tablespoons chopped fresh cilantro**
- **2 tablespoons fresh lime juice**
- **2 cloves garlic, minced**
- **1 tablespoon chili powder**
- **1 teaspoon ground cumin**
- **½ teaspoon salt**
- **1 small green bell pepper, cut into strips**
- **1 small red bell pepper, cut into strips**
- **Flour tortillas, warmed**

1. Cut steak lengthwise in half, then crosswise into thin strips; place meat in **CROCK-POT®** slow cooker. Combine onion, ½ cup salsa, cilantro, lime juice, garlic, chili powder, cumin and salt in **CROCK-POT®** slow cooker. Cover; cook on LOW 5 to 6 hours.

2. Add bell peppers. Cover; cook 1 hour.

3. Serve with flour tortillas and additional salsa, if desired.

Makes 4 servings

Nutrition Information

Calories	200
Total Fat	7g
Saturated Fat	3g
Protein	26g
Carbohydrate	9g
Cholesterol	35mg
Fiber	2g
Sodium	490mg

Dietary Exchanges:
1½ Vegetable, 3½ Meat

Tip

CROCK-POT® slow cooker recipes calling for raw meats should cook a minimum of 3 hours on low for food safety reasons. When in doubt, use an instant-read thermometer to ensure the meat has reached the recommended internal temperature for safe consumption.

Pork Main Dishes

Pork and Mushroom Ragoût

- Nonstick cooking spray
- 1 boneless pork loin roast (1¼ pounds)
- 1¼ cups canned crushed tomatoes, divided
- 2 tablespoons cornstarch
- 2 teaspoons dried savory
- 3 sun-dried tomatoes (not packed in oil), chopped
- 1 package (8 ounces) sliced fresh mushrooms
- 1 large onion, sliced
- 1 teaspoon black pepper
- 3 cups hot cooked noodles

1. Spray large nonstick skillet with nonstick cooking spray; heat over medium heat. Brown roast on all sides; set aside.

2. Place ½ cup crushed tomatoes, cornstarch, savory and sun-dried tomatoes in **CROCK-POT®** slow cooker; mix well. Layer mushrooms, onion and pork over tomato mixture.

3. Pour remaining ¾ cup crushed tomatoes over pork; sprinkle with pepper. Cover; cook on LOW 4 to 6 hours.

4. Transfer roast to cutting board; tent with foil. Let stand 10 to 15 minutes. Slice roast. Serve with sauce over hot cooked noodles.

Makes 6 servings

Nutrition Information

Calories	275
Total Fat	7g
Saturated Fat	2g
Protein	21g
Carbohydrate	33g
Cholesterol	68mg
Fiber	3g
Sodium	169mg

Dietary Exchanges:
1 Vegetable, 2 Starch, 2 Meat

Nutrition Information

Calories	217
Total Fat	9g
Saturated Fat	3g
Protein	23g
Carbohydrate	10g
Cholesterol	72mg
Fiber	1g
Sodium	300mg

Dietary Exchanges:
1 Fruit, 3 Meat

Seared Pork Roast with Currant Cherry Salsa

1½ teaspoons chili powder

¾ teaspoon salt

½ teaspoon garlic powder

½ teaspoon paprika

¼ teaspoon ground allspice

1 boneless pork loin roast (2 pounds)

Nonstick cooking spray

½ cup water

1 package (1 pound) pitted dark cherries, thawed, drained and halved

¼ cup currants or dark raisins

1 teaspoon grated orange peel

1 teaspoon balsamic vinegar

⅛ to ¼ teaspoon red pepper flakes

1. Combine chili powder, salt, garlic powder, paprika and allspice in small bowl. Coat roast evenly with spice mixture, pressing spices into roast.

2. Spray large nonstick skillet with nonstick cooking spray; heat over medium-high heat. Brown roast on all sides. Place in **CROCK-POT®** slow cooker.

3. Pour water into skillet, stirring to scrape up brown bits. Pour liquid into **CROCK-POT®** slow cooker around roast. Cover; cook on LOW 6 to 8 hours.

4. Remove roast from **CROCK-POT®** slow cooker. Tent with foil; keep warm. Strain juices from **CROCK-POT®** slow cooker into small saucepan; discard solids. Keep warm over low heat.

5. Turn **CROCK-POT®** slow cooker to HIGH. Add cherries, currants, orange peel, vinegar and red pepper flakes to **CROCK-POT®** slow cooker. Cover; cook 30 minutes. Slice pork and spoon warm juices over meat. Serve with salsa.

Makes 8 servings

Nutrition Information

Calories	200
Total Fat	6g
Saturated Fat	2g
Protein	26g
Carbohydrate	7g
Cholesterol	70mg
Fiber	<1g
Sodium	520mg

Dietary Exchanges:
1 Vegetable, 3 Meat

Peppered Pork Cutlets with Onion Gravy

- ½ **teaspoon paprika**
- ¼ **teaspoon ground cumin**
- ⅛ **teaspoon ground red pepper (optional)**
- ¼ **teaspoon black pepper**
- 4 **boneless pork cutlets (4 ounces each), trimmed of fat**
  Nonstick cooking spray
- 2 **cups thinly sliced onions**
- 2 **tablespoons flour, divided**
- ¾ **cup water**
- 1½ **teaspoons chicken bouillon granules**
- 2 **tablespoons fat-free (skim) milk**
- ¼ **teaspoon salt**

1. Combine paprika, cumin, ground red pepper, if desired, and black pepper in small bowl; mix well. Sprinkle mixture evenly over one side of each cutlet and press down gently to adhere. Let stand 15 minutes to absorb flavors.

2. Spray large nonstick skillet with nonstick cooking spray; heat over medium heat. Add pork, seasoned side down, and cook 3 minutes or until richly browned. Remove from skillet and transfer to **CROCK-POT®** slow cooker.

3. Spray skillet with nonstick cooking spray; heat over medium-high heat. Add onions; cook and stir 4 minutes or until richly browned. Sprinkle with 1½ tablespoons flour; toss to coat. Stir in water and bouillon, bring to a boil. Add onions and accumulated juices to **CROCK-POT®** slow cooker; spoon sauce over pork. Cover; cook on LOW 4 to 5 hours.

4. Remove pork; set aside. Turn **CROCK-POT®** slow cooker to HIGH. Stir milk into onion mixture, or for thicker consistency, whisk milk into remaining ½ tablespoon flour in small bowl and add to onion mixture. Add salt; cook 10 minutes or until thickened. Spoon sauce over pork.

Makes 4 servings

Nutrition Information

Calories	243
Total Fat	8g
Saturated Fat	3g
Protein	19g
Carbohydrate	23g
Cholesterol	40mg
Fiber	1g
Sodium	191mg

Dietary Exchanges:
1½ Fruit, 2 Meat, 1 Fat

Apple-Cherry Glazed Pork Chops

- ½ to 1 teaspoon dried thyme
- ¼ teaspoon salt
- ¼ teaspoon black pepper
- 4 boneless pork loin chops (3 ounces each), trimmed of fat
  Nonstick cooking spray
- 1⅓ cups unsweetened apple juice
- 1 small apple, sliced
- 4 tablespoons sliced green onion
- 4 tablespoons dried tart cherries
- 2 tablespoons water
- 2 teaspoons cornstarch

1. Combine thyme, salt and pepper in small bowl. Rub onto both sides of pork chops. Spray large nonstick skillet with nonstick cooking spray; heat over medium-high heat. Brown both sides of pork, cooking in batches, if necessary. Transfer to **CROCK-POT®** slow cooker.

2. Add apple juice, apple slices, green onion and cherries to skillet. Simmer 2 to 3 minutes or until apple and onion are tender. Whisk water into cornstarch in small bowl until smooth; stir into skillet. Bring to a boil; cook and stir until thickened. Spoon over pork chops.

3. Cover; cook on LOW 3½ to 4 hours or until pork chops are tender. Serve pork chops with sauce.

Makes 4 servings

Nutrition Information

Calories	209
Total Fat	2g
Saturated Fat	1g
Protein	19g
Carbohydrate	25g
Cholesterol	36mg
Fiber	3g
Sodium	427mg

Dietary Exchanges:
1½ Starch, 2 Meat

Spiced Pork and Apple Stew

- 1 teaspoon canola oil
- 1¼ pounds lean pork stew meat, trimmed of fat, cut into 1-inch pieces
- 1 medium sweet onion, cut into ½-inch-thick slices
- 2 cloves garlic, minced
- 1 can (about 28 ounces) crushed tomatoes
- 1½ cups baby carrots, cut into ½-inch pieces
- 2 large or 3 small red or white potatoes, cut into 1-inch pieces
- 2 small apples, cored and cubed
- 1 cup reduced-sodium chicken broth
- 2 tablespoons spicy brown mustard
- 1 tablespoon brown sugar
- 2 teaspoons ground cinnamon
- 1 teaspoon ground cumin
- ¼ teaspoon salt
- 2 tablespoons chopped fresh Italian parsley (optional)

1. Heat oil in a large nonstick skillet over medium-high heat. Add pork; brown on all sides. Add onion and garlic; reduce heat to medium. Cover; cook and stir 5 minutes. Transfer to **CROCK-POT**® slow cooker.

2. Add remaining ingredients except parsley to **CROCK-POT**® slow cooker. Cover; cook on LOW 6 to 8 hours or until pork and potatoes are tender. Garnish with parsley.

Makes 8 servings

Nutrition Information

Calories	275
Total Fat	10g
Saturated Fat	2g
Protein	28g
Carbohydrate	19g
Cholesterol	65mg
Fiber	1g
Sodium	394mg

Dietary Exchanges:
1 Starch, 4 Meat

Cherry & Mushroom Stuffed Pork Chops

- **2 tablespoons vegetable oil, divided**
- **1 cup chopped fresh shiitake mushrooms**
- **¼ cup finely chopped onion**
- **¼ cup finely chopped celery**
- **¼ cup dried sweetened cherries, chopped**
- **¼ teaspoon salt**
- **⅛ teaspoon dried thyme**
- **⅛ teaspoon black pepper**
- **4 boneless pork loin chops (about 1¼ pounds), cut 1 inch thick**
- **1 teaspoon all-purpose flour**
- **¼ cup fat-free reduced-sodium chicken broth**
- **¼ cup cherry juice**

1. Heat 1 tablespoon oil in large nonstick skillet over medium-high heat. Add mushrooms, onion and celery; cook and stir over medium-high heat 4 minutes. Stir in cherries, salt, thyme and pepper. Transfer mixture to small bowl; set aside.

2. Brown pork chops in skillet about 2 minutes on each side. Cook in two batches, if necessary; set aside. Remove pork from skillet. Drain fat. Add flour to skillet; cook and stir 30 seconds. Stir in broth and juice, stirring to scrape up browned bits. Cook 1 minute to thicken sauce slightly.

3. Cut deep pocket in side of each pork chop; fill with one fourth of cherry stuffing. Skewer pockets closed with toothpicks. Arrange pork chops in **CROCK-POT®** slow cooker, pocket side up. Pour sauce from skillet around pork chops. Cover; cook on LOW 4 to 5 hours or until pork chops are tender. Remove toothpicks before serving.

Makes 4 servings

Nutrition Information

Calories	230
Total Fat	11g
Saturated Fat	3g
Protein	20g
Carbohydrate	12g
Cholesterol	60mg
Fiber	2g
Sodium	280mg

Dietary Exchanges:
½ Starch, 2½ Meat, 1 Fat

Tip

To reduce the amount of fat in **CROCK-POT®** slow cooker meals, trim excess fat from meats.

Jerk Pork and Sweet Potato Stew

- 3 **tablespoons all-purpose flour**
- ¼ **teaspoon salt**
- ¼ **teaspoon black pepper**
- 1¼ **pounds lean pork shoulder, cut into bite-size pieces**
- 2 **tablespoons vegetable oil**
- 1 **large sweet potato, peeled and diced**
- 1 **cup frozen or canned corn**
- ¼ **cup minced green onions (green parts only), divided**
- 1 **clove garlic, minced**
- 1 **medium jalapeño pepper or Scotch bonnet chile, minced (about 1 teaspoon)***
- ⅛ **teaspoon ground allspice**
- 1 **cup fat-free reduced-sodium chicken broth**
- 1 **tablespoon lime juice**
- 2 **cups cooked rice (optional)**

Jalapeño peppers and Scotch bonnet chiles can sting and irritate the skin, so wear rubber gloves when handling and do not touch your eyes.

1. Combine flour, salt and pepper in resealable plastic food storage bag. Add pork and shake well to coat. Heat oil in large nonstick skillet over medium heat. Add pork in a single layer and brown on both sides, about 5 minutes. Cook in 2 batches, if necessary. Transfer to **CROCK-POT®** slow cooker.

2. Add sweet potato, corn, 2 tablespoons green onions, garlic, jalapeño pepper and allspice. Stir in broth. Cover; cook on LOW 5 to 6 hours.

3. Stir in lime juice and remaining 2 tablespoons green onions. Serve stew over cooked rice, if desired.

Makes 6 servings

Nutrition Information

Calories	190
Total Fat	10g
Saturated Fat	3g
Protein	21g
Carbohydrate	18g
Cholesterol	57mg
Fiber	<1g
Sodium	184mg

Dietary Exchanges:
1 Starch, 2½ Meat

Apple Stuffed Pork Loin Roast

- **1 tablespoon butter**
- **2 large tart apples, peeled, cored and thinly sliced (about 2 cups)**
- **1 medium onion, cut into thin strips (about 1 cup)**
- **2 tablespoons packed brown sugar**
- **1 teaspoon Dijon mustard**
- **2 cloves garlic, minced**
- **1 teaspoon coarse salt**
- **1 teaspoon dried rosemary**
- **½ teaspoon dried thyme**
- **½ teaspoon black pepper**
- **1 boneless center cut pork loin roast (4 to 5 pounds)**
- **Nonstick cooking spray**
- **1 cup apple cider or apple juice**

1. Melt butter in large nonstick skillet over medium-high heat. Add apples and onion; cook and stir 5 minutes or until softened. Stir in brown sugar and mustard; set aside.

2. Combine garlic, salt, rosemary, thyme and pepper in small bowl. Cut lengthwise down roast almost to, but not through, bottom. Open like a book. Rub half of garlic mixture onto cut sides of pork.

3. Spread apple and onion mixture evenly onto one cut side of roast. Close halves; tie roast with kitchen string at 2-inch intervals.

4. Coat **CROCK-POT®** slow cooker with nonstick cooking spray. Place roast in **CROCK-POT®** slow cooker. Pour apple cider over roast. Rub outside of roast with remaining garlic mixture. Cover; cook on LOW 5 to 6 hours or on HIGH 2 to 3 hours or until roast is tender.

5. Transfer roast to cutting board and let stand 10 minutes before slicing.

Makes 14 to 16 servings

Nutrition Information

Calories	210
Total Fat	6g
Saturated Fat	2g
Protein	26g
Carbohydrate	12g
Cholesterol	65mg
Fiber	1g
Sodium	170mg

Dietary Exchanges:
½ Fruit, 3 Meat, ½ Fat

Tip

If your pepper mill doesn't produce a coarse grind, you can place whole peppercorns in a plastic bag and use a rolling pin to crush and grind them neatly.

Spicy Citrus Pork with Pineapple Salsa

Nonstick cooking spray

1 **tablespoon ground cumin**

1 **teaspoon coarsely ground black pepper**

½ **teaspoon salt**

3 **pounds lean center-cut pork loin, rinsed and patted dry**

2 **tablespoons vegetable oil**

4 **cans (8 ounces each) pineapple tidbits in own juice, drained, ½ cup juice reserved***

3 **tablespoons lemon juice, divided**

1 **cup finely chopped orange or red bell pepper**

4 **tablespoons finely chopped red onion**

2 **tablespoons chopped fresh cilantro or mint**

2 **teaspoons grated lemon peel**

1 **teaspoon grated fresh ginger (optional)**

¼ **teaspoon red pepper flakes (optional)**

*If tidbits are unavailable, purchase pineapple chunks and coarsely chop.

1. Coat **CROCK-POT®** slow cooker with nonstick cooking spray. Combine cumin, black pepper and salt in small bowl; rub evenly onto pork. Heat oil in medium nonstick skillet over medium-high heat. Brown pork loin 1 to 2 minutes per side. Transfer to **CROCK-POT®** slow cooker.

2. Spoon 4 tablespoons of reserved pineapple juice and 2 tablespoons lemon juice over pork. Cover; cook on LOW 2 to 2¼ hours or on HIGH 1 to 1½ hours or until pork is tender.

3. Meanwhile, combine pineapple, remaining 4 tablespoons pineapple juice, remaining 1 tablespoon lemon juice, bell pepper, onion, cilantro, lemon peel, ginger and red pepper flakes, if desired, in medium bowl; set aside.

4. Transfer pork to serving platter. Let pork stand 10 minutes before slicing. Arrange pork slices on serving platter. Serve with salsa.

Makes 12 servings

Nutrition Information

Calories	170
Total Fat	6g
Saturated Fat	2g
Protein	25g
Carbohydrate	2g
Cholesterol	73mg
Fiber	<1g
Sodium	189mg

Dietary Exchanges:
3 Meat, ½ Fat

Pork Roast with Dijon Tarragon Glaze

1½ **to 2 pounds boneless pork loin, visible fat removed**

½ **teaspoon black pepper**

1 **teaspoon ground paprika**

⅓ **cup reduced-sodium chicken or vegetable broth**

2 **tablespoons Dijon mustard**

2 **tablespoons lemon juice**

1 **teaspoon minced fresh tarragon**

1. Sprinkle roast with pepper and paprika. Place roast in **CROCK-POT®** slow cooker. Combine broth, mustard, lemon juice and tarragon in small bowl; spoon over roast. Cover; cook on LOW 6 to 8 hours or on HIGH 3 to 4 hours.

2. Remove roast from **CROCK-POT®** slow cooker; let stand 15 minutes before slicing.

Makes 4 to 6 servings

Stew Provençal

- **2 cans (about 14 ounces each) fat-free reduced-sodium beef broth, divided**
- **⅓ cup all-purpose flour**
- **1 to 2 lean pork tenderloins (about 2 pounds), trimmed and cut into 1-inch pieces**
- **4 medium red potatoes, unpeeled, cut into cubes**
- **2 cups frozen cut green beans, thawed**
- **1 medium onion, chopped**
- **2 cloves garlic, minced**
- **1 teaspoon salt**
- **1 teaspoon dried thyme**
- **½ teaspoon black pepper**

1. Combine ¾ cup beef broth and flour in small bowl; cover and refrigerate.

2. Combine remaining broth, pork, potatoes, green beans, onion, garlic, salt, thyme and pepper in **CROCK-POT®** slow cooker; mix well. Cover; cook on LOW 8 to 10 hours or on HIGH 4 to 5 hours.

3. Stir flour mixture into **CROCK-POT®** slow cooker. Cook, uncovered, 30 minutes or until thickened.

Makes 8 servings

Nutrition Information	
Calories	240
Total Fat	3g
Saturated Fat	1g
Protein	28g
Carbohydrate	24g
Cholesterol	75mg
Fiber	3g
Sodium	560mg

Dietary Exchanges:
½ Vegetable, 2½ Meat

Nutrition Information

Calories................................ 250
Total Fat...............................9g
Saturated Fat......................3g
Protein 30g
Carbohydrate.....................9g
Cholesterol....................95mg
Fiber......................................1g
Sodium.........................610mg

Dietary Exchanges:
1½ Vegetable, 4 Meat,
½ Fat

Rough-Cut Smoky Red Pork Roast

Nonstick cooking spray

1 **lean pork shoulder roast (about 3¼ pounds)**

1 **can (about 14 ounces) stewed tomatoes, drained**

1 **can (6 ounces) tomato paste with basil, oregano and garlic**

1 **cup chopped red bell pepper**

2 **to 3 canned chipotle peppers in adobo sauce, finely chopped and mashed with fork***

1 **teaspoon salt**

1½ **to 2 tablespoons sugar**

For less heat, remove seeds from chipotle peppers before mashing.

1. Coat **CROCK-POT®** slow cooker with nonstick cooking spray. Place pork, fat side up, on bottom. Combine remaining ingredients except sugar in small bowl. Pour over pork. Cover; cook on HIGH 5 hours.

2. Transfer pork to cutting board; let stand 15 minutes before slicing. Stir sugar into cooking liquid. Cook, uncovered, 15 minutes. Serve pork with sauce.

Makes 10 servings

Asian Pork Tenderloin

- ½ **cup bottled garlic ginger sauce**
- ¼ **cup sliced green onions**
- 1 **pork tenderloin (about 1 pound)**
- 1 **large red onion, cut into chunks**
- 1 **medium red bell pepper, cut into 1-inch pieces**
- 1 **medium zucchini, cut into ¼ inch slices**
- 1 **tablespoon olive oil**

1. Place sauce and green onions in large resealable food storage bag. Add pork; seal bag and turn to coat. Refrigerate 30 minutes or overnight.

2. Combine onion, bell pepper, zucchini and oil in large bowl; toss to coat. Place vegetables in **CROCK-POT®** slow cooker. Remove pork from bag and place on top of vegetables. Discard marinade. Cover; cook on LOW 6 to 7 hours or on HIGH 4 to 5 hours.

3. Transfer pork to cutting board; loosely cover with foil and let stand 10 minutes before slicing. Serve pork with vegetables.

Makes 4 servings

Nutrition Information

Calories	220
Total Fat	5g
Saturated Fat	2g
Protein	24g
Carbohydrate	15g
Cholesterol	75mg
Fiber	1g
Sodium	540mg

Dietary Exchanges:
1 Vegetable, 3 Meat

Heavenly Harvest Pork Roast

¼ **cup pomegranate juice**

¼ **cup sugar**

1 **teaspoon salt**

1 **tablespoon garlic salt**

1 **tablespoon steak seasoning**

1 **teaspoon black pepper**

1 **lean pork loin roast (2¾ pounds)**

2 **pears, cored, peeled and sliced thick**

2 **oranges with peel, sliced thick**

1. Combine pomegranate juice and sugar in small saucepan. Cook over low heat, stirring until sugar dissolves, about 2 minutes. Pour into **CROCK-POT®** slow cooker.

2. Blend salt, garlic salt, steak seasoning and pepper in small mixing bowl. Rub mixture over roast. Place roast in **CROCK-POT®** slow cooker. Turn roast to cover with juice mixture.

3. Top roast with pear and orange slices. Cover; cook on HIGH 6 to 8 hours or until tender. Serve with juice and fruit slices.

Makes 10 servings

Barbecued Pulled Pork Sandwiches

1 lean pork shoulder roast (2½ pounds)

1 bottle (14 ounces) barbecue sauce

1 tablespoon fresh lemon juice

1 teaspoon packed brown sugar

1 medium onion, chopped

Hamburger buns or hard rolls

1. Place pork roast in **CROCK-POT®** slow cooker. Cover; cook on LOW 10 to 12 hours or on HIGH 5 to 6 hours.

2. Remove pork roast from **CROCK-POT®** slow cooker. Shred with two forks. Discard cooking liquid. Return pork to **CROCK-POT®** slow cooker; add barbecue sauce, lemon juice, brown sugar and onion. Cover and cook on LOW 2 hours or on HIGH 1 hour. Serve pork by itself or on hamburger buns or hard rolls.

Makes 8 servings

Nutrition Information

Calories	230
Total Fat	9g
Saturated Fat	3g
Protein	17g
Carbohydrate	20g
Cholesterol	60mg
Fiber	1g
Sodium	600mg

Dietary Exchanges:
2½ Meat, 1 Fat, 1 Other

Tip

For a 5-, 6- or 7-quart **CROCK-POT®** slow cooker, double all ingredients, except for the barbecue sauce. Increase the barbecue sauce to 1½ bottles (about 21 ounces total).

Nutrition Information

Calories.................................277
Total Fat..............................4g
Saturated Fat.......................1g
Protein 24g
Carbohydrate.....................21g
Cholesterol..................66mg
Fiber.......................................1g
Sodium..........................145mg

Dietary Exchanges:
1 Vegetable, ½ Fruit, 3 Meat

Pork Tenderloin with Cabbage

3 cups shredded red cabbage
¼ cup chopped onion
1 clove garlic, minced
¼ cup chicken broth or water
1½ pounds pork tenderloin
¾ cup apple juice concentrate
3 tablespoons honey mustard
1½ tablespoons Worcestershire sauce

1. Combine cabbage, onion and garlic in **CROCK-POT**® slow cooker; pour in broth. Place pork over cabbage mixture. Combine apple juice concentrate, mustard and Worcestershire sauce in small bowl; pour over pork. Cover; cook on LOW 6 to 8 hours or on HIGH 3 to 4 hours.

2. Slice pork and serve with cabbage and juices.

Makes 6 servings

Simple Shredded Pork Tacos

1¾ pounds lean boneless pork roast

1 cup salsa

1 can (4 ounces) chopped green chiles

½ teaspoon garlic salt

½ teaspoon black pepper

Flour or corn tortillas, warmed

Optional toppings: salsa, sour cream, diced tomatoes, shredded cheese, shredded lettuce

1. Combine roast, salsa, chiles, garlic salt and pepper in **CROCK-POT®** slow cooker. Cover; cook on LOW 8 hours or until meat is tender.

2. Remove pork from **CROCK-POT®** slow cooker; shred with two forks. Serve on flour tortillas with sauce. Top as desired.

Makes 6 servings

Nutrition Information

Calories 190
Total Fat 4g
Saturated Fat 1.5g
Protein 30g
Carbohydrate 4g
Cholesterol 75mg
Fiber 1g
Sodium 370mg

Dietary Exchanges:
½ Vegetable, 4 Meat

Tip

Cut the pork roast to fit in the bottom of your **CROCK-POT®** slow cooker in one or two layers.

Nutrition Information

Calories	190
Total Fat	8g
Saturated Fat	3g
Protein	12g
Carbohydrate	18g
Cholesterol	25mg
Fiber	2g
Sodium	570mg

Dietary Exchanges:
1 Starch, 1½ Meat, 1 Fat

Ham and Potato Casserole

- 1½ **pounds red potatoes, peeled and sliced**
- 8 **ounces thinly sliced lean ham**
- 2 **poblano chile peppers, cut into thin strips**
- 2 **tablespoons olive oil**
- 1 **tablespoon dried oregano**
- ¼ **teaspoon salt**
- 1 **cup (4 ounces) shredded reduced-fat Monterey Jack or Pepper-Jack cheese**
- 2 **tablespoons finely chopped fresh cilantro**

1. Combine all ingredients except cheese and cilantro in **CROCK-POT®** slow cooker; mix well. Cover; cook on LOW 7 hours or on HIGH 4 hours.

2. Transfer potato mixture to serving dish; sprinkle with cheese and cilantro. Let stand 3 minutes or until cheese is melted.

Makes 7 servings

Chili Verde

Nonstick cooking spray

¾ **pound boneless lean pork, cut into 1-inch cubes**

1 **pound fresh tomatillos, husks removed, coarsely chopped**

1 **can (about 15 ounces) Great Northern beans, rinsed and drained**

1 **can (about 14 ounces) fat-free reduced-sodium chicken broth**

1 **large onion, halved and thinly sliced**

1 **can (4 ounces) diced mild green chiles**

6 **cloves garlic, chopped or sliced**

1 **teaspoon ground cumin**

½ **cup lightly packed fresh cilantro, chopped**

1. Spray large nonstick skillet with nonstick cooking spray; heat over medium-high heat. Add pork; cook until browned on all sides.

2. Combine pork and all remaining ingredients except cilantro in **CROCK-POT®** slow cooker. Cover; cook on HIGH 3 to 4 hours.

3. Turn **CROCK-POT®** slow cooker to LOW. Stir in cilantro and cook 10 minutes.

Makes 4 servings

Nutrition Information

Calories	250
Total Fat	4g
Saturated Fat	1g
Protein	26g
Carbohydrate	28g
Cholesterol	55mg
Fiber	10g
Sodium	680mg

Dietary Exchanges:
2½ Vegetable, 1 Starch, 2½ Meat

Nutrition Information

Calories	90
Total Fat	3g
Saturated Fat	1g
Protein	14g
Carbohydrate	1g
Cholesterol	40mg
Fiber	0g
Sodium	520mg

Dietary Exchanges:
2 Meat

Variation

Mu Shu Pork: Lightly spread prepared plum sauce over small warm flour tortillas. Spoon ¼ cup pork filling and ¼ cup stir-fried vegetables into flour tortillas. Wrap to enclose. Serve immediately. Makes about 20 wraps.

Spicy Asian Pork Filling

  1 **lean boneless pork sirloin roast (about 3 pounds)**

  ½ **cup low sodium soy sauce**

  1 **tablespoon chili paste or chili garlic sauce**

  2 **teaspoons minced fresh ginger**

  2 **tablespoons water**

  1 **tablespoon cornstarch**

  2 **teaspoons dark sesame oil**

1. Cut roast into 2- to 3-inch chunks. Combine pork, soy sauce, chili paste and ginger in **CROCK-POT®** slow cooker; mix well. Cover; cook on LOW 8 to 10 hours or until pork is fork-tender.

2. Remove roast from cooking liquid; cool slightly. Trim and discard excess fat. Shred pork with two forks. Let cooking liquid stand 5 minutes to allow fat to rise. Skim off and discard fat.

3. Whisk water, cornstarch and sesame oil in small bowl until smooth; stir into cooking liquid. Turn **CROCK-POT®** slow cooker to HIGH. Cook, uncovered, 10 minutes or until thickened. Return pork to **CROCK-POT®** slow cooker; mix well. Cover; cook 15 to 30 minutes or until heated through.

Makes 5½ cups

Simple Slow Cooker Pork Roast

1 marinated lean pork loin roast (2³⁄₄ pounds)*

4 to 5 medium red potatoes, cut into bite-size pieces

4 medium carrots, cut into bite-size pieces

¹⁄₂ cup water

1 package (10 ounces) frozen baby peas

Salt and black pepper, to taste

If marinated roast is unavailable, prepare marinade by mixing ¹⁄₄ cup olive oil, 1 tablespoon minced garlic and 1¹⁄₂ tablespoons Italian seasoning. Place in large resealable plastic food storage bag with pork roast. Marinate in refrigerator at least 2 hours or overnight.

1. Combine pork roast, potatoes and carrots in **CROCK-POT**® slow cooker. (If necessary, cut roast in half to fit.) Add water. Cover; cook on LOW 6 to 8 hours or until vegetables are tender.

2. Add peas during last hour of cooking. Transfer pork to serving platter. Season with salt and pepper, if desired. Slice and serve with vegetables.

Makes 10 servings

Nutrition Information	
Calories	320
Total Fat	12g
Saturated Fat	3g
Protein	30g
Carbohydrate	20g
Cholesterol	70mg
Fiber	3g
Sodium	100mg

Dietary Exchanges:
¹⁄₂ Vegetable, 1 Starch, 4 Meat, 1 Fat

Nutrition Information

Calories	217
Total Fat	7g
Saturated Fat	2g
Protein	22g
Carbohydrate	20g
Cholesterol	54mg
Fiber	3g
Sodium	89mg

Dietary Exchanges:
1 Starch, 3 Meat

Pork in Chile Sauce

- **2 large tomatoes, chopped**
- **2 cups no-salt-added tomato purée**
- **2 small poblano chiles, cored, seeded and chopped**
- **2 large shallots or 1 small onion, chopped**
- **2 cloves garlic, minced**
- **¼ teaspoon chipotle chili powder or regular chili powder***
- **½ teaspoon dried oregano**
- **¼ teaspoon black pepper**
- **2 (6-ounce) boneless pork chops, cut into 1-inch chunks**
- **½ teaspoon salt (optional)**
- **4 corn or whole wheat tortillas, warmed (optional)**

Chipotle chili powder is available in the spice section of many supermarkets.

Combine tomatoes, tomato purée, poblano chiles, shallots, garlic, chili powder, oregano and black pepper in **CROCK-POT®** slow cooker; mix well. Add pork. Cover; cook on LOW 5 to 6 hours. Stir in salt, if desired. Serve in tortillas, if desired.

Makes 4 servings

Orange Teriyaki Pork

Nonstick cooking spray
1 **pound lean pork stew meat, cut into 1-inch cubes**
1 **package (16 ounces) frozen stir-fry pepper blend**
4 **ounces sliced water chestnuts**
½ **cup orange juice**
2 **tablespoons quick-cooking tapioca**
2 **tablespoons packed light brown sugar**
2 **tablespoons teriyaki sauce**
½ **teaspoon ground ginger**
½ **teaspoon dry mustard**
1⅓ **cups hot cooked rice**

1. Spray large nonstick skillet with nonstick cooking spray; heat over medium heat. Add pork; brown on all sides. Remove from heat; set aside.

2. Place peppers and water chestnuts in **CROCK-POT®** slow cooker. Top with pork. Combine orange juice, tapioca, brown sugar, teriyaki sauce, ginger and mustard in large bowl. Pour in **CROCK-POT®** slow cooker. Cover; cook on LOW 3 to 4 hours. Serve with rice.

Makes 4 servings

Nutrition Information	
Calories	313
Total Fat	6g
Saturated Fat	2g
Protein	21g
Carbohydrate	42g
Cholesterol	49mg
Fiber	4g
Sodium	406mg

Dietary Exchanges:
2 Vegetable, 2 Starch, 2 Meat

Poultry Main Dishes

White Bean Chili

Nonstick cooking spray

1 **pound ground chicken**

3 **cups coarsely chopped celery**

1 **can (about 28 ounces) whole tomatoes, undrained and coarsely chopped**

1 **can (about 15 ounces) Great Northern beans, rinsed and drained**

1½ **cups coarsely chopped onions**

1 **cup chicken broth**

3 **cloves garlic, minced**

4 **teaspoons chili powder**

1½ **teaspoons ground cumin**

¾ **teaspoon ground allspice**

¾ **teaspoon ground cinnamon**

½ **teaspoon black pepper**

1. Spray large nonstick skillet with nonstick cooking spray; brown chicken over medium-high heat, stirring to break up meat.

2. Combine chicken, celery, tomatoes, beans, onions, broth, garlic, chili powder, cumin, allspice, cinnamon and pepper in **CROCK-POT®** slow cooker. Cover; cook on LOW 5½ to 6 hours.

Makes 6 servings

Nutrition Information

Calories	148
Total Fat	2g
Saturated Fat	1g
Protein	15g
Carbohydrate	21g
Cholesterol	26mg
Fiber	7g
Sodium	657mg

Dietary Exchanges:
1 Vegetable, 1 Starch, 1 Meat

Nutrition Information

Calories.....................140
Total Fat.........................5g
Saturated Fat........................1g
Protein 10g
Carbohydrate.....................15g
Cholesterol....................25mg
Fiber.................................1g
Sodium.........................280mg

Dietary Exchanges:
1 Vegetable, ½ Starch,
1 Meat, ½ Fat

Mini Meatball Grinders

- **1 can (about 14 ounces) diced tomatoes, drained and juices reserved**
- **1 can (8 ounces) no-salt-added tomato sauce**
- **¼ cup chopped onion**
- **2 tablespoons tomato paste**
- **1 teaspoon Italian seasoning**
- **1 pound ground chicken**
- **½ cup fresh whole wheat or white bread crumbs (1 slice bread)**
- **1 egg white, lightly beaten**
- **3 tablespoons finely chopped fresh parsley**
- **2 cloves garlic, minced**
- **¼ teaspoon salt**
- **⅛ teaspoon black pepper**
- **Nonstick cooking spray**
- **4 hard rolls, split and toasted**
- **3 tablespoons grated Parmesan cheese**

1. Combine diced tomatoes, ½ cup reserved juice, tomato sauce, onion, tomato paste and Italian seasoning in **CROCK-POT®** slow cooker. Cover; cook on LOW 3 to 4 hours.

2. Halfway through cooking time, prepare meatballs. Combine chicken, bread crumbs, egg white, parsley, garlic, salt and pepper in medium bowl. With wet hands, shape mixture into 12 balls. Place meatballs on clean plate. Cover and refrigerate 30 minutes.

3. Spray medium nonstick skillet with nonstick cooking spray; heat over medium heat. Add meatballs; cook about 8 to 10 minutes or until well browned on all sides. Transfer to **CROCK-POT®** slow cooker. Cover; cook 1 to 2 hours or until meatballs are cooked through (165°F).

4. Place 3 meatballs in each roll. Spoon sauce over meatballs and sprinkle with cheese. Cut each roll into 3 smaller sandwiches, 1 meatball per smaller sandwich, holding mini grinders together with cocktail picks, if desired.

Makes 12 servings

Nutrition Information

Calories	250
Total Fat	8g
Saturated Fat	3g
Protein	19g
Carbohydrate	24g
Cholesterol	45mg
Fiber	2g
Sodium	780mg

Dietary Exchanges:
½ Vegetable, 1 Starch,
2 Meat, 1 Fat

Greek Chicken Pitas with Creamy Mustard Sauce

Filling

Nonstick cooking spray

1 **medium green bell pepper, seeded and sliced into ½-inch strips**

1 **medium onion, cut into 8 wedges**

½ **pound boneless, skinless chicken breasts, rinsed and patted dry**

1 **tablespoon extra virgin olive oil**

2 **teaspoons dried Greek seasoning blend**

¼ **teaspoon salt**

Sauce

¼ **cup fat-free plain yogurt**

¼ **cup fat-free mayonnaise**

1 **tablespoon prepared mustard**

4 **whole pita rounds**

½ **cup reduced-fat crumbled feta cheese**

Optional toppings: sliced cucumbers, sliced tomatoes, kalamata olives

1. Coat **CROCK-POT®** slow cooker with nonstick cooking spray. Place bell pepper and onion in bottom. Add chicken and drizzle with oil. Sprinkle evenly with Greek seasoning and salt. Cover; cook on HIGH 1¾ hours or until chicken is cooked through (165°F) and vegetables are crisp-tender.

2. Whisk yogurt, mayonnaise, and mustard in small bowl until smooth.

3. Remove chicken from **CROCK-POT®** slow cooker and slice. Remove vegetables using slotted spoon. Warm pitas according to package directions. Cut in half; layer with chicken, sauce, vegetables and cheese. Top as desired.

Makes 4 servings

Indian-Style Apricot Chicken

Nutrition Information	
Calories	280
Total Fat	11g
Saturated Fat	3g
Protein	23g
Carbohydrate	29g
Cholesterol	90mg
Fiber	3g
Sodium	460mg

Dietary Exchanges:
1 Vegetable, 1½ Fruit,
3 Meat, ½ Fat

Nonstick cooking spray

6 skinless chicken thighs, rinsed and patted dry

¼ teaspoon salt

¼ teaspoon black pepper

1 tablespoon vegetable oil

1 large onion, chopped

2 cloves garlic, minced

2 tablespoons grated fresh ginger

½ teaspoon ground cinnamon

⅛ teaspoon ground allspice

1 can (about 14 ounces) diced tomatoes

1 cup fat-free chicken broth

1 package (8 ounces) dried apricots

1 pinch saffron threads (optional)

Hot basmati rice

2 tablespoons chopped fresh Italian parsley (optional)

1. Coat **CROCK-POT**® slow cooker with nonstick cooking spray. Season chicken with salt and pepper. Heat oil in large skillet over medium-high heat. Brown chicken on all sides. Transfer to **CROCK-POT**® slow cooker.

2. Add onion to skillet; cook and stir 3 to 5 minutes or until translucent. Add garlic, ginger, cinnamon and allspice; cook and stir 15 to 30 seconds or until mixture is fragrant. Add tomatoes and broth; cook 2 to 3 minutes or until mixture is heated through. Pour into **CROCK-POT**® slow cooker.

3. Add apricots and saffron, if desired. Cover; cook on LOW 5 to 6 hours or on HIGH 3 to 4 hours or until chicken is tender. Serve with rice and garnish with parsley.

Makes 6 servings

Nutrition Information

Calories.................................313
Total Fat.................................3g
Saturated Fat......................1g
Protein 30g
Carbohydrate...................41g
Cholesterol..................100mg
Fiber...3g
Sodium..........................123mg

Dietary Exchanges:
2 Starch, 3 Meat

Turkey Stroganoff

Nonstick cooking spray

4 cups sliced mushrooms

2 stalks celery, thinly sliced

2 medium shallots *or* **½ small onion, minced**

1 cup reduced-sodium chicken broth

½ teaspoon dried thyme

¼ teaspoon black pepper

2 turkey tenderloins, turkey breasts or boneless, skinless chicken thighs (about 10 ounces each), cut into bite-size chunks

½ cup fat-free sour cream

1 tablespoon plus 1 teaspoon all-purpose flour

¼ teaspoon salt (optional)

1⅓ cups hot cooked cholesterol-free whole wheat egg noodles

1. Spray large nonstick skillet with nonstick cooking spray. Add mushrooms, celery and shallots; cook and stir over medium heat 5 minutes or until mushrooms and shallots are tender. Spoon into **CROCK-POT®** slow cooker. Stir in broth, thyme and pepper. Stir in turkey; mix well. Cover; cook on LOW 5 to 6 hours.

2. Combine sour cream and flour in small bowl. Spoon 2 tablespoons cooking liquid from **CROCK-POT®** slow cooker into bowl; stir well. Stir sour cream mixture into slow cooker. Cover; cook 10 minutes. Stir in salt, if desired.

3. Serve turkey with sauce over noodles.

Makes 4 servings

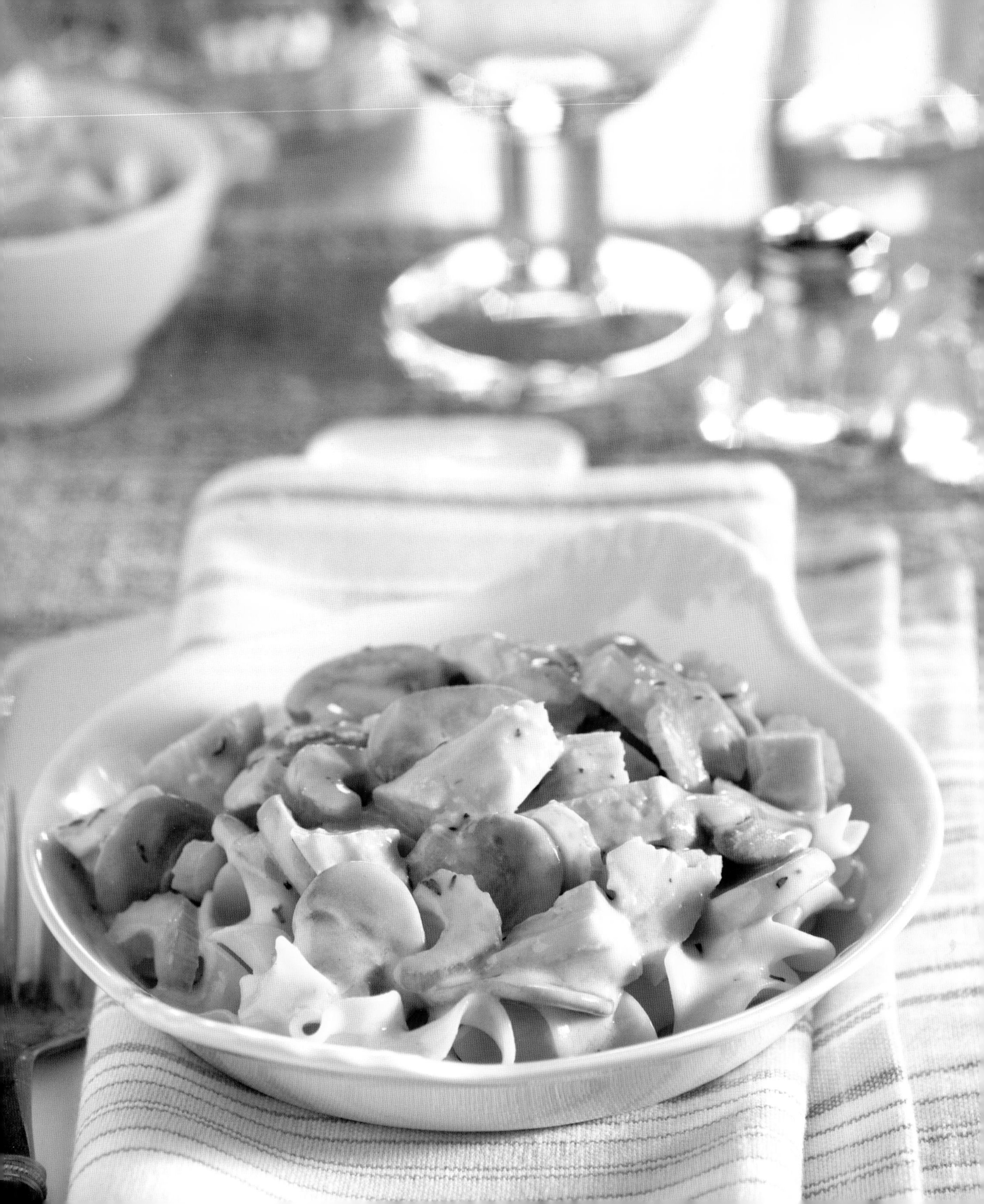

Nutrition Information

Calories................................342
Total Fat................................11g
Saturated Fat.......................2g
Protein.................................23g
Carbohydrate....................32g
Cholesterol..................94mg
Fiber...2g
Sodium..........................105mg

Dietary Exchanges:
1 Vegetable, 2 Starch, 3 Meat

Tip

Don't peek!
The **CROCK-POT**® slow cooker can take as long as 30 minutes to regain heat lost when the cover is removed. Only remove the cover when instructed to do so by the recipe.

Moroccan Chicken Stew

- **1 pound boneless, skinless chicken thighs, cut into 2-inch pieces**
- **½ to ¾ cup white wine**
- **½ cup chopped celery**
- **⅓ cup white balsamic vinegar**
- **½ cup chopped carrots**
- **2 ounces chopped prunes**
- **¼ cup packed brown sugar**
- **2 tablespoons olive oil**
- **3 cloves garlic, minced**
- **3 bay leaves**
- **½ teaspoon ground cinnamon**
- **½ teaspoon ground coriander**
- **¼ teaspoon dried oregano**
- **Pinch black pepper**
- **Pinch ground ginger**

Place all ingredients in **CROCK-POT**® slow cooker. Cover and cook on LOW 3 to 4 hours. Remove and discard bay leaves before serving.

Makes 4 servings

Nutrition Information

Calories	137
Total Fat	4g
Saturated Fat	1g
Protein	7g
Carbohydrate	18g
Cholesterol	19mg
Fiber	1g
Sodium	206mg

Dietary Exchanges:
1 Fruit, 1 Meat, ½ Fat

Turkey Meatballs in Cranberry-Barbecue Sauce

- **1 can (16 ounces) jellied cranberry sauce**
- **½ cup barbecue sauce**
- **1 egg white**
- **1 pound 93% lean ground turkey**
- **1 green onion, sliced**
- **2 teaspoons grated orange peel**
- **1 teaspoon reduced-sodium soy sauce**
- **¼ teaspoon black pepper**
- **⅛ teaspoon ground red pepper (optional)**
- **Nonstick cooking spray**

1. Combine cranberry sauce and barbecue sauce in **CROCK-POT®** slow cooker. Cover; cook on HIGH 20 to 30 minutes or until cranberry sauce is melted and mixture is heated through.

2. Meanwhile, place egg white in medium bowl; beat lightly. Add turkey, green onion, orange peel, soy sauce, black pepper and ground red pepper, if desired; mix until well blended. Shape into 24 balls.

3. Spray large nonstick skillet with nonstick cooking spray. Add meatballs to skillet; cook over medium heat 8 to 10 minutes or until meatballs are browned on all sides and cooked through (165°F).

4. Place meatballs in **CROCK-POT®** slow cooker; stir gently to coat evenly with sauce. Turn **CROCK-POT®** slow cooker to LOW. Cover; cook 3 hours.

Makes 12 servings

Nutrition Information

Calories	226
Total Fat	3g
Saturated Fat	<1g
Protein	19g
Carbohydrate	31g
Cholesterol	60mg
Fiber	5g
Sodium	156mg

Dietary Exchanges:
2 Starch, 2 Meat

Chicken Goulash

- **2 small onions, chopped**
- **2 stalks celery, chopped**
- **2 medium carrots, chopped**
- **1 clove garlic, minced**
- **1 cup reduced-sodium chicken broth**
- **1 cup no-salt-added tomato purée**
- **2 teaspoons paprika**
- **½ teaspoon dried marjoram or oregano**
- **¼ teaspoon black pepper**
- **10 ounces boneless, skinless chicken thighs, trimmed and cut-into bite-size pieces**
- **2 small unpeeled new potatoes, diced**
- **2 heaping teaspoons all-purpose flour**
- **½ teaspoon salt (optional)**

1. Combine onions, celery, carrots and garlic in **CROCK-POT®** slow cooker. Combine broth, tomato purée, paprika, marjoram and pepper in small bowl; pour over vegetables. Add chicken and potatoes. Cover; cook on LOW 5 to 6 hours.

2. Whisk flour into 2 tablespoons cooking liquid in small bowl. Stir flour mixture into **CROCK-POT®** slow cooker. Cover; cook 10 minutes. Stir in salt, if desired.

Makes 4 servings

Sweet Chicken Curry

1 pound boneless, skinless chicken breasts, cut into 1-inch pieces

1 large green or red bell pepper, cut into 1-inch pieces

1 large onion, sliced

1 large tomato, seeded and chopped

½ cup prepared mango chutney

¼ cup water

2 tablespoons cornstarch

1½ teaspoons curry powder

Hot cooked rice

1. Combine chicken, bell pepper and onion in **CROCK-POT®** slow cooker. Top with tomato.

2. Combine chutney, water, cornstarch and curry powder in small bowl; pour over chicken. Cover; cook on LOW 3½ to 4½ hours or until chicken is tender. Serve over rice.

Makes 4 servings

Nutrition Information

Calories	210
Total Fat	7g
Saturated Fat	1g
Protein	26g
Carbohydrate	7g
Cholesterol	75mg
Fiber	1g
Sodium	490mg

Dietary Exchanges:
1 Vegetable, 3 Meat, ½ Fat

Autumn Chicken

- **1 can (14 ounces) whole artichoke hearts, drained**
- **1 can (14 ounces) whole mushrooms, divided**
- **12 boneless, skinless chicken breasts**
- **1 jar (6½ ounces) marinated artichoke hearts, undrained**
- **¾ cup white wine**
- **½ cup balsamic vinaigrette**
- **Hot cooked noodles**
- **Paprika for garnish (optional)**

Spread whole artichokes over bottom of **CROCK-POT®** slow cooker. Top with half of mushrooms. Layer chicken over mushrooms. Add marinated artichoke hearts with liquid. Add remaining mushrooms. Pour in wine and vinaigrette. Cover; cook on LOW 4 to 5 hours. Serve over noodles. Garnish with paprika, if desired.

Makes 12 servings

Turkey Vegetable Chili Mac

Nonstick cooking spray

¾ **pound extra-lean ground turkey breast**

1 **can (about 15 ounces) black beans, rinsed and drained**

1 **can (about 14 ounces) Mexican-style diced tomatoes**

1 **can (about 14 ounces) no-salt-added diced tomatoes**

1 **cup frozen corn**

½ **cup chopped onion**

2 **cloves garlic, minced**

1 **teaspoon Mexican seasoning**

½ **cup (about 2 ounces) uncooked elbow macaroni**

⅓ **cup sour cream**

1. Spray large nonstick skillet with nonstick cooking spray; heat over medium heat. Add turkey; cook until browned. Transfer to **CROCK-POT®** slow cooker. Add beans, tomatoes, corn, onion, garlic and Mexican seasoning. Cover; cook on LOW 4 to 5 hours.

2. Stir in macaroni. Cover; cook 10 minutes. Stir. Cover; cook 20 to 30 minutes or until pasta is tender. Serve with sour cream.

Makes 6 servings

Nutrition Information

Calories	210
Total Fat	4g
Saturated Fat	2g
Protein	20g
Carbohydrate	24g
Cholesterol	30mg
Fiber	5g
Sodium	340mg

Dietary Exchanges:
1½ Vegetable, 1 Starch,
1½ Meat, ½ Fat

Tip

Feel free to substitute 2 ounces of any other pasta. Short pasta shapes like cavatappi, penne or rigatoni can be added straight out of the packages. Longer shapes such as linguine, fettuccine or spaghetti should be broken in halves or thirds before being stirred in so that all the pasta can be fully immersed in the sauce.

Nutrition Information

Calories.................................170
Total Fat.................................5g
Saturated Fat.........................1g
Protein...................................20g
Carbohydrate.......................11g
Cholesterol..........................55mg
Fiber...2g
Sodium.............................570mg

Dietary Exchanges:
½ Vegetable, ½ Starch,
2 Meat, ½ Fat, ½ Other

Boneless Chicken Cacciatore

- **1 tablespoon olive oil**
- **6 boneless, skinless chicken breasts, sliced in half horizontally**
- **4 cups reduced-sodium tomato-basil sauce or marinara sauce**
- **1 cup coarsely chopped yellow onion**
- **1 cup coarsely chopped green bell pepper**
- **1 can (6 ounces) sliced mushrooms**
- **¼ cup dry red wine (optional)**
- **2 teaspoons minced garlic**
- **2 teaspoons dried oregano, crushed**
- **2 teaspoons dried thyme, crushed**
- **1 teaspoon salt**
- **2 teaspoons black pepper**

1. Heat oil in skillet over medium heat until hot. Brown chicken on both sides, turning as it browns. Drain and transfer to **CROCK-POT®** slow cooker.

2. Add remaining ingredients, and stir well to combine. Cover; cook on LOW 5 to 7 hours or on HIGH 2 to 3 hours.

Makes 8 servings

Hoisin Barbecue Chicken Sliders

- ⅔ **cup hoisin sauce**
- ⅓ **cup barbecue sauce**
- 3 **tablespoons quick-cooking tapioca**
- 1 **tablespoon sugar**
- 1 **tablespoon reduced-sodium soy sauce**
- ¼ **teaspoon red pepper flakes**
- 12 **boneless, skinless chicken thighs (3 to 3½ pounds total)**
- 16 **dinner rolls or Hawaiian sweet rolls, split**
- ½ **medium red onion, finely chopped**
- **Sliced pickles (optional)**

1. Combine hoisin sauce, barbecue sauce, tapioca, sugar, soy sauce and red pepper flakes in **CROCK-POT®** slow cooker; mix well. Add chicken. Cover; cook on LOW 8 to 9 hours.

2. Remove cooked chicken from sauce and chop or shred with two forks. Return chopped chicken and any sauce that may accumulate to **CROCK-POT®** slow cooker to keep warm until serving. Serve generous ¼ cup chicken and sauce on each roll. Top with 1 teaspoon chopped red onion and pickles, if desired.

Makes 16 sliders

Nutrition Information

Calories	280
Total Fat	8g
Saturated Fat	3g
Protein	22g
Carbohydrate	35g
Cholesterol	75mg
Fiber	1g
Sodium	500mg

Dietary Exchanges:
2 Starch, ½ Other, 2 Meat

Nutrition Information

Calories	203
Total Fat	1g
Saturated Fat	<1g
Protein	36g
Carbohydrate	10g
Cholesterol	99mg
Fiber	1g
Sodium	70mg

Dietary Exchanges:
½ Vegetable, ½ Fruit,
4½ Meat

Herbed Turkey Breast with Orange Sauce

1 **large onion, chopped**

3 **cloves garlic, minced**

1 **teaspoon dried rosemary**

½ **teaspoon black pepper**

1 **boneless, skinless turkey breast (3 pounds)**

1½ **cups orange juice**

1. Place onion in **CROCK-POT®** slow cooker. Combine garlic, rosemary and pepper in small bowl; set aside.

2. Cut slices about three-fourths of the way through turkey at 2-inch intervals. Rub garlic mixture between slices. Place turkey, cut side up, in **CROCK-POT®** slow cooker. Pour orange juice over turkey. Cover; cook on LOW 7 to 8 hours.

3. Serve sliced turkey with orange sauce.

Makes 4 to 6 servings

Italian Stew

1 **can (about 14 ounces) chicken broth**

1 **can (about 14 ounces) Italian stewed tomatoes with peppers and onions, undrained**

1 **package (9 ounces) fully cooked spicy chicken sausage, sliced**

2 **carrots, thinly sliced**

2 **small zucchini, sliced**

1 **can (16 ounces) Great Northern, cannellini or navy beans, rinsed and drained**

2 **tablespoons chopped fresh basil (optional)**

1. Combine all ingredients except beans and basil in **CROCK-POT®** slow cooker. Cover; cook on LOW 6 to 7 hours or on HIGH 3 to 4 hours or until vegetables are tender.

2. Turn **CROCK-POT®** slow cooker to HIGH. Stir in beans. Cover; cook 10 to 15 minutes or until beans are heated through. Serve with basil, if desired.

Makes 4 servings

Nutrition Information	
Calories	293
Total Fat	7g
Saturated Fat	2g
Protein	24g
Carbohydrate	38g
Cholesterol	46mg
Fiber	8g
Sodium	134mg

Dietary Exchanges:
2½ Starch, 2 Meat

Nutrition Information

Calories	90
Total Fat	3g
Saturated Fat	1g
Protein	8g
Carbohydrate	5g
Cholesterol	30mg
Fiber	1g
Sodium	250mg

Dietary Exchanges:
1 Vegetable

Chipotle Turkey Sloppy Joe Sliders

- **1 pound turkey Italian sausage, casings removed**
- **1 bag (14 ounces) frozen green and red pepper strips with onions**
- **1 can (6 ounces) tomato paste**
- **1 tablespoon quick-cooking tapioca**
- **1 tablespoon minced chipotle pepper in adobo sauce, plus 1 tablespoon sauce**
- **2 teaspoons ground cumin**
- **½ teaspoon dried thyme**
- **Corn muffins or small dinner rolls, split and toasted**

1. Brown sausage in medium nonstick skillet over medium-high heat, stirring frequently to break up meat. Drain fat. Transfer to **CROCK-POT®** slow cooker.

2. Stir pepper strips, tomato paste, tapioca, chipotle pepper and sauce, cumin and thyme into **CROCK-POT®** slow cooker. Cover; cook on LOW 8 to 10 hours. Serve on corn muffins.

Makes 12 sliders

Provençal Lemon and Olive Chicken

- **2 cups chopped onion**
- **2 pounds skinless chicken thighs**
- **1 medium lemon, thinly sliced and seeds removed**
- **½ cup pitted green olives**
- **1 tablespoon white vinegar or olive brine from jar**
- **2 teaspoons herbes de Provence**
- **1 bay leaf**
- **½ teaspoon salt**
- **⅛ teaspoon black pepper**
- **1 cup fat-free reduced-sodium chicken broth**
- **½ cup minced fresh Italian parsley**

Place onion in **CROCK-POT®** slow cooker. Arrange chicken thighs over onion. Place lemon slice on each thigh. Add olives, vinegar, herbes de Provence, bay leaf, salt and pepper. Slowly pour in chicken broth. Cover; cook on LOW 5 to 6 hours or on HIGH 3 to 3½ hours or until chicken is tender. Remove and discard bay leaf. Sprinkle with parsley before serving.

Makes 10 servings

Nutrition Information	
Calories	150
Total Fat	10g
Saturated Fat	3g
Protein	18g
Carbohydrate	5g
Cholesterol	75mg
Fiber	1g
Sodium	400mg

Dietary Exchanges:
½ Vegetable, 2 Meat, ½ Fat

Chicken and Sweet Potato Stew

Nutrition Information	
Calories	200
Total Fat	2g
Saturated Fat	0g
Protein	20g
Carbohydrate	26g
Cholesterol	50mg
Fiber	5g
Sodium	600mg

Dietary Exchanges:
2 Vegetable, 1 Starch, 2 Meat

Tip

Recipe can be doubled for a 5-, 6- or 7-quart **CROCK-POT®** slow cooker.

- **4 boneless, skinless chicken breasts, cut into bite-size pieces**
- **2 medium sweet potatoes, peeled and cubed**
- **2 medium Yukon Gold potatoes, peeled and cubed**
- **2 medium carrots, peeled and cut into ½-inch slices**
- **1 can (28 ounces) reduced-sodium whole stewed tomatoes**
- **1 teaspoon salt**
- **1 teaspoon paprika**
- **1 teaspoon celery seeds**
- **½ teaspoon freshly ground black pepper**
- **⅛ teaspoon ground cinnamon**
- **⅛ teaspoon ground nutmeg**
- **1 cup fat-free reduced-sodium chicken broth**
- **¼ cup fresh basil, chopped**

Combine all ingredients except basil in **CROCK-POT®** slow cooker. Cover; cook on LOW 6 to 8 hours or on HIGH 3 to 4 hours. Sprinkle with basil just before serving.

Makes 6 servings

Creamy Chicken Sausage Rice Pilaf

- **3 cups water**
- **1 package (12 ounces) fully cooked chicken apple sausage, cut into ½-inch slices**
- **3 medium carrots, chopped**
- **1 medium onion, chopped**
- **½ cup brown basmati rice**
- **1 box (4 ounces) wild rice**
- **½ cup sweetened dried cranberries**
- **1 teaspoon dried oregano**
- **¾ teaspoon salt**
- **¼ teaspoon black pepper**
- **½ cup half-and-half or whipping cream**

Combine all ingredients except half-and-half in **CROCK-POT®** slow cooker. Cover; cook on LOW 7 to 8 hours or until rice is tender. Turn off heat. Stir in half-and-half and let stand 10 minutes before serving.

Makes 8 servings

Nutrition Information	
Calories	230
Total Fat	8g
Saturated Fat	3g
Protein	10g
Carbohydrate	31g
Cholesterol	55mg
Fiber	3g
Sodium	580mg

Dietary Exchanges:
½ Fruit, 1 Starch, 2 Meat, 1 Fat

Nutrition Information

Calories..................................248
Total Fat................................4g
Saturated Fat......................1g
Protein..................................17g
Carbohydrate....................36g
Cholesterol....................30mg
Fiber.......................................3g
Sodium.........................282mg

Dietary Exchanges:
1 Vegetable, 1 Fruit,
½ Starch, 2 Meat

Tip

To slightly thicken a sauce in the **CROCK-POT®** slow cooker, remove the solid foods and leave the sauce in the **CROCK-POT®** slow cooker. Mix 1 to 2 tablespoons cornstarch with ¼ cup cold water until smooth. Stir mixture into the sauce and cook on HIGH until the sauce is thickened.

Mu Shu Turkey

1 **can (16 ounces) plums, drained and pitted**
½ **cup orange juice**
¼ **cup finely chopped onion**
1 **tablespoon minced fresh ginger**
¼ **teaspoon ground cinnamon**
1 **pound boneless, turkey breast, cut into thin strips**
6 **(7-inch) flour tortillas, warmed**
3 **cups coleslaw mix**

1. Place plums in blender or food processor; process until almost smooth. Combine plums, orange juice, onion, ginger and cinnamon in **CROCK-POT®** slow cooker; mix well. Place turkey over plum mixture. Cover; cook on LOW 3 to 4 hours.

2. Remove turkey from **CROCK-POT®** slow cooker. Divide evenly among tortillas. Spoon about 2 tablespoons plum sauce over turkey in each tortilla; top with about ½ cup coleslaw mix. Fold up bottom edges of tortillas over filling, fold in sides and roll up to enclose filling. Use remaining plum sauce for dipping.

Makes 6 servings

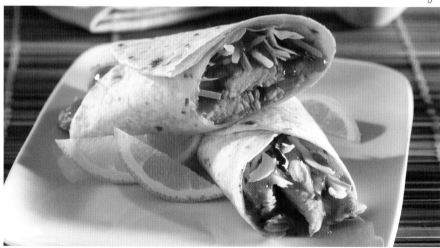

Chicken Sausage with Peppers & Basil

- **1 tablespoon olive oil**
- **½ medium yellow onion, minced (about ½ cup)**
- **1 clove garlic, minced**
- **1 pound sweet or hot Italian chicken sausage**
- **1 can (28 ounces) whole tomatoes, drained and seeded**
- **½ medium red bell pepper, cut into ½-inch slices**
- **½ medium yellow bell pepper, cut into ½-inch slices**
- **½ medium orange bell pepper, cut into ½-inch slices**
- **¾ cup chopped fresh basil**
- **Crushed red pepper flakes, to taste**
- **Salt and black pepper, to taste**
- **Hot cooked pasta**

1. Heat oil in large skillet over medium heat. Add onion and garlic and cook until translucent.

2. Remove sausage from casing and cut into 1-inch chunks. Add to skillet and cook 3 to 4 minutes or until just beginning to brown. Transfer to **CROCK-POT®** slow cooker with slotted spoon, skimming off some fat.

3. Add tomatoes, bell peppers, basil, pepper flakes, salt and black pepper to **CROCK-POT®** slow cooker and stir to blend. Cook on HIGH 2½ to 3 hours or until bell peppers have softened. Adjust seasonings to taste. Serve over pasta.

Makes 6 servings

Nutrition Information

Calories	170
Total Fat	8g
Saturated Fat	2g
Protein	14g
Carbohydrate	8g
Cholesterol	60mg
Fiber	2g
Sodium	650mg

Dietary Exchanges:
1½ Vegetable, 2 Meat, 1 Fat

Nutrition Information

Calories	157
Total Fat	3g
Saturated Fat	1g
Protein	14g
Carbohydrate	14g
Cholesterol	41mg
Fiber	<1g
Sodium	93mg

Dietary Exchanges:
1 Fruit, 2 Meat

Sweet Jalapeño Mustard Turkey Thighs

3 turkey thighs, skin removed

¾ cup honey mustard

½ cup orange juice

1 tablespoon cider vinegar

1 teaspoon Worcestershire sauce

1 to 2 fresh jalapeño peppers, finely chopped*

1 clove garlic, minced

½ teaspoon grated orange peel

*Jalapeño peppers can sting and irritate the skin, so wear rubber gloves when handling peppers and do not touch your eyes.

Place turkey thighs in single layer in **CROCK-POT®** slow cooker. Combine remaining ingredients in large bowl. Pour mixture over turkey thighs. Cover; cook on LOW 5 to 6 hours.

Makes 6 servings

Citrus Mangoretto Chicken

4 boneless, skinless chicken breasts (about 1 pound)

1 large ripe mango, peeled and diced

3 tablespoons freshly squeezed lime juice

1 tablespoon grated lime peel

¼ cup Amaretto liqueur

1 tablespoon chopped fresh rosemary or 1 teaspoon crushed dried rosemary

1 cup fat-free chicken broth

1 tablespoon water

2 teaspoons cornstarch

1. Place 2 chicken breasts side by side on bottom of **CROCK-POT®** slow cooker.

2. Combine mango, lime juice, lime peel, Amaretto and rosemary in medium bowl. Spread half of mango mixture over chicken in **CROCK-POT®** slow cooker. Lay remaining 2 chicken breasts on top crosswise, and spread with remaining mango mixture. Carefully pour broth around edges of chicken. Cover; cook on LOW 3 to 4 hours.

3. Combine water and cornstarch. Stir into cooking liquid. Cook 15 minutes longer or until sauce has thickened. Serve mango and sauce over chicken.

Makes 4 servings

Nutrition Information

Calories	210
Total Fat:	4g
Saturated Fat:	1g
Protein	25g
Carbohydrate	16g
Cholesterol	75mg
Fiber	1g
Sodium	370mg

Dietary Exchanges:
½ Fruit, 3 Meat

Variation

Chill chicken and sauce. Serve over salad greens.

Vegetarian Main Dishes

Curried Lentils with Fruit

- **5 cups water**
- **1½ cups uncooked lentils, rinsed, sorted and drained***
- **1 Granny Smith apple, cored, peeled and chopped**
- **¼ cup golden raisins**
- **¼ cup fat-free lemon yogurt**
- **1 teaspoon curry powder**
- **1 teaspoon salt**

*Packages of dried lentils may contain grit and tiny stones. Therefore, thoroughly rinse lentils, then sort through and discard grit or any unusual looking pieces.

1. Combine water, lentils, apple and raisins in **CROCK-POT®** slow cooker. Cover; cook on LOW 8 to 9 hours or until lentils are tender. (Lentils should absorb most or all of the water. Slightly tilt **CROCK-POT®** slow cooker to check.)

2. Place lentil mixture in large serving bowl; stir in yogurt, curry powder and salt until well blended.

Makes 6 servings

Nutrition Information

Calories	160
Total Fat	1g
Saturated Fat	<1g
Protein	10g
Carbohydrate	31g
Cholesterol	<1mg
Fiber	6g
Sodium	364mg

Dietary Exchanges:
½ Fruit, 2 Starch

Nutrition Information

Calories	241
Total Fat	7g
Saturated Fat	<1g
Protein	5g
Carbohydrate	43g
Cholesterol	0mg
Fiber	7g
Sodium	470mg

Dietary Exchanges:
3 Starch, 1 Fat

Vegetarian Paella

- **2 teaspoons canola oil**
- **1 cup chopped onion**
- **2 cloves garlic, minced**
- **1 cup brown rice**
- **2¼ cups vegetable broth**
- **1 can (about 14 ounces) no-salt-added stewed tomatoes**
- **1 cup coarsely chopped carrots**
- **1 cup chopped red bell pepper**
- **1 small zucchini, halved lengthwise and sliced to ½-inch thickness (about 1¼ cups)**
- **1 teaspoon Italian seasoning**
- **½ teaspoon ground turmeric**
- **⅛ teaspoon ground red pepper**
- **1 can (14 ounces) quartered artichoke hearts, drained**
- **½ cup frozen baby peas**
- **¾ teaspoon salt (optional)**

1. Heat oil in large nonstick skillet over medium-high heat. Add onion; cook 6 to 7 minutes or until tender. Stir in garlic.

2. Combine rice with onion and garlic in **CROCK-POT®** slow cooker. Add all remaining ingredients but artichokes, peas and salt; mix well. Cover; cook on LOW 4 hours or on HIGH 2 hours, or until liquid is absorbed.

3. Stir in artichokes and peas. Season with salt, if desired. Cover; cook 5 to 10 minutes or until vegetables are tender.

Makes 6 servings

Ratatouille with Parmesan Cheese

Nonstick cooking spray

1 **baby eggplant, diced, or 1 cup diced regular eggplant**

2 **medium tomatoes, chopped**

1 **small zucchini, diced**

1 **cup sliced mushrooms**

½ **cup no-salt-added tomato purée**

1 **large shallot *or* ½ small onion, chopped**

1 **clove garlic, minced**

¾ **teaspoon dried oregano**

⅛ **teaspoon dried rosemary**

⅛ **teaspoon black pepper**

2 **tablespoons shredded fresh basil**

2 **teaspoons lemon juice**

¼ **teaspoon salt (optional)**

¼ **cup shredded Parmesan cheese**

1. Spray large nonstick skillet with nonstick cooking spray. Add eggplant; cook and stir over medium-high heat about 5 minutes or until lightly browned.

2. Transfer eggplant to **CROCK-POT®** slow cooker. Add tomatoes, zucchini, mushrooms, tomato purée, shallot, garlic, oregano, rosemary and pepper. Cover; cook on LOW 6 hours.

3. Stir in basil, lemon juice and salt, if desired. Turn off slow cooker; let stand 5 minutes. Top each serving with 1 tablespoon cheese.

Makes 4 servings

Nutrition Information

Calories	195
Total Fat	5g
Saturated Fat	2g
Protein	9g
Carbohydrate	31g
Cholesterol	9mg
Fiber	4g
Sodium	128mg

Dietary Exchanges:
1 Starch, ½ Meat, 1 Fat

Polenta Lasagna

Nonstick cooking spray

4 **cups boiling water**

1½ **cups whole grain yellow cornmeal**

4 **teaspoons finely chopped fresh marjoram**

1 **teaspoon olive oil**

1 **pound fresh mushrooms, sliced**

1 **cup chopped leeks**

1 **clove garlic, minced**

½ **cup (2 ounces) shredded part-skim mozzarella cheese**

2 **tablespoons chopped fresh basil**

1 **tablespoon chopped fresh oregano**

⅛ **teaspoon black pepper**

2 **medium red bell peppers, chopped**

¼ **cup water**

¼ **cup freshly grated Parmesan cheese, divided**

1. Coat **CROCK-POT®** slow cooker with nonstick cooking spray. Combine 4 cups boiling water and cornmeal in **CROCK-POT®** slow cooker; mix well. Stir in marjoram. Cover; cook on LOW 3 to 4 hours or on HIGH 1 to 2 hours, stirring occasionally. Cover and chill about 1 hour or until firm.

2. Heat oil in medium nonstick skillet over medium heat. Cook and stir mushrooms, leeks and garlic 5 minutes or until leeks are crisp-tender. Stir in mozzarella cheese, basil, oregano and black pepper.

3. Place bell peppers and ¼ cup water in food processor or blender; process until smooth.

4. Cut cold polenta in half and place one half in bottom of **CROCK-POT®** slow cooker. Top with half of bell pepper mixture, half of vegetable mixture and 2 tablespoons Parmesan cheese. Place remaining polenta over Parmesan cheese; layer with remaining bell pepper and vegetable mixtures and Parmesan cheese. Cover; cook on LOW 3 hours or until cheese is melted and polenta is golden brown.

Makes 6 servings

Nutrition Information

Calories	340
Total Fat	9g
Saturated Fat	3g
Protein	14g
Carbohydrate	51g
Cholesterol	10mg
Fiber	9g
Sodium	360mg

Dietary Exchanges:
3½ Vegetable, 1½ Starch,
½ Meat, 1 Fat

Mushroom and Vegetable Ragoût over Polenta

Ragoût

- 3 tablespoons extra virgin olive oil
- 8 ounces sliced mushrooms
- 8 ounces shiitake mushrooms, stemmed and thinly sliced
- ½ cup Madeira wine
- 1 can (about 28 ounces) crushed tomatoes
- 1 can (about 15 ounces) low-sodium chickpeas, rinsed and drained
- 1 medium onion, chopped
- 1 can (about 6 ounces) tomato paste
- 4 cloves garlic, minced
- 1 sprig fresh rosemary

Polenta

- 2 cups reduced-fat (2%) milk
- 2 cups water
- ¼ teaspoon salt
- 2 cup instant polenta
- ½ cup grated Parmesan cheese

1. Heat oil in large nonstick skillet over medium-high heat. Add mushrooms; cook and stir 8 to 10 minutes or until browned. Add Madeira; cook 1 minute until liquid is reduced by approximately half. Transfer to **CROCK-POT®** slow cooker.

2. Stir in tomatoes, chickpeas, onion, tomato paste, garlic and rosemary. Cover; cook on LOW 6 hours or until vegetables are tender. Remove and discard rosemary.

3. Meanwhile, combine milk, water and salt in large saucepan over medium-high heat. Bring to a boil and slowly whisk in polenta in a slow, steady stream. Whisk 4 to 5 minutes or until thick and creamy.

4. Remove polenta from heat and stir in cheese. Top polenta with ragoût.

Makes 8 servings

Nutrition Information

Calories	90
Total Fat	0g
Saturated Fat	0g
Protein	5g
Carbohydrate	19g
Cholesterol	0mg
Fiber	4g
Sodium	770mg

Dietary Exchanges:
3½ Vegetable

Vegetable Pasta Sauce

 2 **cans (about 14 ounces each) diced tomatoes**
 1 **can (about 14 ounces) whole tomatoes, undrained**
1½ **cups sliced mushrooms**
 1 **medium red bell pepper, diced**
 1 **medium green bell pepper, diced**
 1 **small yellow squash, cut into ¼-inch slices**
 1 **small zucchini, cut into ¼-inch slices**
 1 **can (6 ounces) tomato paste**
 4 **green onions, sliced**
 3 **cloves garlic, minced**
 2 **tablespoons Italian seasoning**
 1 **tablespoon chopped Italian parsley**
 1 **teaspoon salt**
 1 **teaspoon red pepper flakes (optional)**
 1 **teaspoon black pepper**
    Hot cooked pasta
    Parmesan cheese and fresh basil (optional)

Combine all ingredients except pasta, cheese and basil in **CROCK-POT®** slow cooker; stir until well blended. Cover; cook on LOW 6 to 8 hours. Serve over cooked pasta. Top with Parmesan cheese and basil, if desired.

Makes 6 servings

Nutrition Information

Calories	290
Total Fat	4g
Saturated Fat	1g
Protein	14g
Carbohydrate	51g
Cholesterol	0mg
Fiber	14g
Sodium	500mg

Dietary Exchanges:
2 Vegetable, 2½ Starch,
½ Fat

Lentil and Spinach Stew

- **1 tablespoon olive oil**
- **3 medium stalks celery, cut into ½-inch pieces**
- **3 medium carrots, cut into ½-inch pieces**
- **1 medium onion, chopped**
- **3 cloves garlic, minced**
- **Nonstick cooking spray**
- **4 cups reduced-sodium vegetable broth**
- **1 can (about 14 ounces) diced tomatoes**
- **1 cup dried brown lentils, sorted, rinsed and drained***
- **2 teaspoons ground cumin**
- **½ teaspoon dried basil**
- **½ teaspoon salt**
- **¼ teaspoon black pepper**
- **5 cups baby spinach**
- **⅓ pound uncooked ditalini pasta**

*Packages of dried lentils may contain grit and tiny stones. Therefore, thoroughly rinse lentils, then sort through and discard grit or any unusual looking pieces.

1. Heat oil in large nonstick skillet over medium-high heat. Add celery, carrots, onion and garlic; cook and stir 3 to 4 minutes or until vegetables begin to soften.

2. Coat **CROCK-POT**® slow cooker with nonstick cooking spray. Transfer vegetable mixture to **CROCK-POT**® slow cooker. Stir in broth, tomatoes, lentils, cumin, basil, salt and pepper. Cover; cook on LOW 8 to 9 hours or until lentils are tender but still hold their shape.

3. Stir in spinach just before serving. Prepare pasta according to package directions. Serve stew over pasta.

Makes 6 servings

Nutrition Information

Calories	156
Total Fat	5g
Saturated Fat	<1g
Protein	7g
Carbohydrate	25g
Cholesterol	0mg
Fiber	5g
Sodium	111mg

Dietary Exchanges:
1 Vegetable, 1 Starch, 1 Fat

Spring Vegetable Ragoût

- **1 tablespoon olive oil**
- **2 leeks, thinly sliced**
- **3 cloves garlic, minced**
- **3 cups small cherry tomatoes, halved**
- **1 package (10 ounces) frozen corn**
- **½ pound yellow squash, halved lengthwise and cut into ½-inch pieces (about 1¼ cups)**
- **1 cup vegetable broth**
- **1 small bag (6 ounces) frozen edamame (soybeans), shelled**
- **1 small bag (4 ounces) shredded carrots**
- **1 teaspoon dried tarragon**
- **1 teaspoon dried basil**
- **1 teaspoon dried oregano**
- **Minced fresh parsley (optional)**

1. Heat oil in large nonstick skillet over medium heat. Add leeks and garlic; cook and stir just until fragrant.

2. Combine leeks and garlic with tomatoes, corn, squash, broth, edamame, carrots, tarragon, basil and oregano in **CROCK-POT®** slow cooker; mix well. Cover; cook on LOW 6 to 8 hours or on HIGH 3 to 4 hours or until vegetables are tender. Garnish with parsley.

Makes 6 servings

Nutrition Information

Calories	252
Total Fat	5g
Saturated Fat	<1g
Protein	12g
Carbohydrate	46g
Cholesterol	0mg
Fiber	7g
Sodium	765mg

Dietary Exchanges:
2 Vegetable, 2½ Starch,
½ Fat

Mexican Hot Pot

- **1 tablespoon canola oil**
- **1 medium onion, chopped**
- **3 cloves garlic, minced**
- **2 teaspoons red pepper flakes**
- **2 teaspoons dried oregano**
- **1 teaspoon ground cumin**
- **1 can (about 28 ounces) whole tomatoes, drained and chopped**
- **2 cups corn**
- **1 can (about 15 ounces) chickpeas, rinsed and drained**
- **1 can (about 15 ounces) pinto beans, rinsed and drained**
- **1 cup water**
- **6 cups shredded iceberg lettuce**

1. Heat oil in large nonstick skillet over medium-high heat. Add onion and garlic; cook and stir 5 minutes. Add red pepper flakes, oregano and cumin; mix well.

2. Transfer onion and garlic mixture to **CROCK-POT®** slow cooker. Stir in tomatoes, corn, chickpeas, pinto beans and water. Cover; cook on LOW 7 to 8 hours or on HIGH 2 to 3 hours.

3. Top each serving with 1 cup shredded lettuce.

Makes 6 servings

Nutrition Information

Calories	248
Total Fat	1g
Saturated Fat	<1g
Protein	11g
Carbohydrate	49g
Cholesterol	0mg
Fiber	11g
Sodium	611mg

Dietary Exchanges:
1 Vegetable, 3 Starch

Red Beans & Rice

- **2 cans (about 15 ounces each) red beans, undrained**
- **1 can (about 14 ounces) diced tomatoes**
- **½ cup chopped celery**
- **½ cup chopped green bell pepper**
- **½ cup chopped green onions**
- **2 cloves garlic, minced**
- **1 to 2 teaspoon hot pepper sauce**
- **1 teaspoon Worcestershire sauce**
- **1 bay leaf**
- **3 cups hot cooked rice**

1. Combine all ingredients except rice in **CROCK-POT®** slow cooker. Cover; cook on LOW 4 to 6 hours or on HIGH 2 to 3 hours.

2. Mash mixture slightly in slow cooker with potato masher until thickened. Turn **CROCK-POT®** slow cooker to HIGH. Cover; cook 30 to 60 minutes. Remove and discard bay leaf before serving. Serve over rice.

Makes 6 servings

Southwestern Beans and Vegetables

1 **can (about 15 ounces) black beans, drained and rinsed**

½ **cup frozen corn**

½ **cup reduced-sodium chicken broth**

1 **large shallot** *or* **½ small onion, finely chopped**

1 **small jalapeño pepper, minced***

1 **clove garlic, minced**

¼ **teaspoon ground cumin**

⅛ **teaspoon black pepper**

1 **tablespoon finely chopped fresh cilantro**

1 **tablespoon lime juice**

¼ **teaspoon salt (optional)**

*Jalapeño peppers can sting and irritate the skin, so wear rubber gloves when handling peppers and do not touch your eyes.

1. Combine beans, corn, broth, shallot, jalapeño pepper, garlic, cumin and black pepper in **CROCK-POT®** slow cooker; mix well. Cover; cook on LOW 5 to 6 hours.

2. Stir in cilantro, lime juice and salt, if desired. Turn off heat; let stand 5 minutes before serving.

Makes 4 servings

Nutrition Information

Calories	84
Total Fat	<1g
Saturated Fat	0g
Protein	5g
Carbohydrate	20g
Cholesterol	<1mg
Fiber	6g
Sodium	421mg

Dietary Exchanges:
1 Starch

Nutrition Information

Calories	230
Total Fat	0g
Saturated Fat	0g
Protein	6g
Carbohydrate	47g
Cholesterol	0mg
Fiber	2g
Sodium	530mg

Dietary Exchanges:
1½ Vegetable, 2 Starch

Artichoke and Tomato Paella

4 **cups reduced-sodium vegetable broth**

2 **cups converted white rice**

5 **ounces (½ 10-ounce package) frozen chopped spinach, thawed and drained**

1 **medium green bell pepper, cored, seeded and chopped**

1 **medium ripe tomato, sliced into wedges**

1 **medium yellow onion, chopped**

1 **medium carrot, peeled and diced**

3 **cloves garlic, minced**

1 **tablespoon minced flat-leaf parsley**

1 **teaspoon salt**

½ **teaspoon black pepper**

1 **can (13¾ ounces) artichoke hearts, quartered, rinsed and well-drained**

½ **cup frozen peas**

1. Combine broth, rice, spinach, bell pepper, tomato, onion, carrot, garlic, parsley, salt and pepper in **CROCK-POT®** slow cooker. Mix thoroughly. Cover; cook on LOW 4 hours or on HIGH 2 hours.

2. Before serving, add artichoke hearts and peas. Cover; cook on HIGH 15 minutes. Mix well before serving.

Makes 8 servings

Manchego Eggplant

- **4 large eggplants**
- **1 cup all-purpose flour**
- **2 tablespoons olive oil**
- **1 jar (25½ ounces) roasted garlic flavor pasta sauce, divided**
- **2 tablespoons Italian seasoning, divided**
- **3½ ounces grated manchego cheese, divided**
- **1 jar (24 ounces) roasted eggplant flavor marinara, divided**

1. Peel eggplants and slice horizontally into ¾-inch-thick pieces. Place flour in shallow bowl. Dredge each slice of eggplant in flour to coat.

2. Heat oil in large skillet over medium-high heat. In batches, lightly brown eggplant on both sides.

3. Pour thin layer of roasted garlic flavor pasta sauce into bottom of **CROCK-POT®** slow cooker. Top with eggplant slices, Italian seasoning, manchego cheese and roasted eggplant flavor marinara. Repeat layers until all ingredients have been used.

4. Cover and cook on HIGH 2 hours.

Makes 8 to 10 servings

Nutrition Information

Calories	90
Total Fat	4g
Saturated Fat	0g
Protein	2g
Carbohydrate	13g
Cholesterol	0mg
Fiber	3g
Sodium	520mg

Dietary Exchanges:
1½ Vegetable, ½ Fat

Slow Cooker Veggie Stew

- **1 tablespoon vegetable oil**
- **¾ cup carrot slices**
- **½ cup diced onion**
- **2 cloves garlic, chopped**
- **2 cans (about 14 ounces each) fat-free vegetable broth**
- **1½ cups chopped green cabbage**
- **½ cup cut green beans**
- **½ cup diced zucchini**
- **1 tablespoon tomato paste**
- **½ teaspoon dried basil**
- **½ teaspoon dried oregano**
- **¼ teaspoon salt**

1. Heat oil in medium nonstick skillet over medium-high heat. Add carrot, onion and garlic; cook and stir until tender.

2. Transfer carrot mixture to **CROCK-POT®** slow cooker. Add remaining ingredients, mix well. Cover; cook on LOW 8 to 10 hours or on HIGH 4 to 5 hours.

Makes 4 to 6 servings

Black Bean Stuffed Peppers

- **1 medium onion, finely chopped**
- **Nonstick cooking spray**
- **¼ teaspoon ground red pepper**
- **¼ teaspoon dried oregano**
- **¼ teaspoon ground cumin**
- **¼ teaspoon chili powder**
- **1 can (15 ounces) black beans, rinsed and drained**
- **6 tall green bell peppers, tops removed, seeded and cored**
- **1 cup (4 ounces) shredded reduced-fat Monterey Jack cheese**
- **1 cup tomato salsa**
- **½ cup fat-free sour cream**

1. Cook onion in medium skillet, sprayed with cooking spray, until golden. Add the ground red pepper, oregano, cumin and chili powder.

2. Mash half of black beans with cooked onion in medium bowl. Stir in remaining beans. Place bell peppers in **CROCK-POT®** slow cooker; spoon black bean mixture into bell peppers. Sprinkle cheese over peppers. Pour salsa over cheese. Cover; cook on LOW 6 to 8 hours or on HIGH 3 to 4 hours.

3. Serve each pepper with a dollop of sour cream.

Makes 6 servings

Nutrition Information

Calories	180
Total Fat	5g
Saturated Fat	3g
Protein	11g
Carbohydrate	25g
Cholesterol	10mg
Fiber	6g
Sodium	550mg

Dietary Exchanges:
2 Vegetable, 1 Starch, 2 Meat

Tip

You may increase any of the recipe ingredients to taste except the tomato salsa, and use a 5-, 6- or 7-quart **CROCK-POT®** slow cooker. However, the peppers should fit comfortably in a single layer in your stoneware.

Nutrition Information

Calories	300
Total Fat	12g
Saturated Fat	2g
Protein	8g
Carbohydrate	43g
Cholesterol	0mg
Fiber	10g
Sodium	750mg

Dietary Exchanges:
1 Vegetable, 2 Starch, 2 Fat

Asian Golden Barley with Cashews

- **2 tablespoons olive oil**
- **1 cup hulled barley, sorted**
- **3 cups vegetable broth**
- **1 cup chopped celery**
- **1 medium green bell pepper, cored, seeded and chopped**
- **1 medium yellow onion, peeled and minced**
- **1 clove garlic, minced**
- **¼ teaspoon black pepper**
- **1 ounce finely chopped cashews**

1. Heat skillet over medium heat until hot. Add olive oil and barley. Cook and stir about 10 minutes or until barley is slightly browned. Transfer to **CROCK-POT®** slow cooker.

2. Add broth, celery, bell pepper, onion, garlic and black pepper. Stir well to combine. Cover; cook on LOW 4 to 5 hours or on HIGH 2 to 3 hours, or until barley is tender and liquid is absorbed.

3. To serve, garnish with cashews.

Makes 4 servings

Chunky Italian Stew with White Beans

- **2 teaspoons olive oil**
- **4 green bell peppers, cut into ¾-inch pieces (about 1¼ pounds total)**
- **2 yellow squash, cut into ¾-inch pieces**
- **2 zucchini, cut into ¾-inch pieces**
- **2 onions, cut into ¾-inch pieces**
- **8 ounces mushrooms, quartered (about 2 cups)**
- **2 cans (about 15 ounces) reduced-sodium navy beans, rinsed and drained**
- **2 cans (about 14 ounces) reduced-sodium diced tomatoes**
- **2 teaspoons dried oregano**
- **1 teaspoon sugar**
- **1 teaspoon Italian seasoning**
- **¼ teaspoon red pepper flakes (optional)**
- **1½ cups (6 ounces) shredded part-skim mozzarella cheese**
- **2 tablespoons grated Parmesan cheese**

1. Heat oil in large nonstick skillet over medium-high heat. Add bell peppers, squash, zucchini, onions and mushrooms; cook and stir 8 minutes or until onion is translucent.

2. Combine vegetables with beans, tomatoes, oregano, sugar, Italian seasoning and red pepper flakes, if desired, in **CROCK-POT®** slow cooker. Cover; cook on LOW 7 to 8 hours.

3. Top with cheeses just before serving.

Makes 8 servings

Nutrition Information

Calories	265
Total Fat	6g
Saturated Fat	3g
Protein	17g
Carbohydrate	38g
Cholesterol	15mg
Fiber	9g
Sodium	208mg

Dietary Exchanges:
1 Vegetable, 2 Starch, 2 Meat, 1 Fat

Variation

Instead of couscous, serve stew over cooked quinoa.

Lentil Stew over Couscous

- **3 cups dried lentils (1 pound), sorted and rinsed**
- **3 cups water**
- **1 can (about 14 ounces) fat-free reduced-sodium chicken broth**
- **1 can (about 14 ounces) diced tomatoes**
- **1 large onion, chopped**
- **1 green bell pepper, chopped**
- **4 stalks celery, chopped**
- **1 medium carrot, halved lengthwise and sliced**
- **2 cloves garlic, chopped**
- **1 teaspoon dried marjoram**
- **¼ teaspoon black pepper**
- **1 tablespoon olive oil**
- **1 tablespoon cider vinegar**
- **4½ to 5 cups hot cooked couscous**

1. Combine lentils, water, broth, tomatoes, onion, bell pepper, celery, carrot, garlic, marjoram and black pepper in **CROCK-POT®** slow cooker; mix well. Cover and cook on LOW 8 to 9 hours or until vegetables are tender.

2. Stir in oil and vinegar. Serve over couscous.

Makes 12 servings

Three-Bean Chipotle Chili

2 tablespoons olive oil

1 large onion, chopped

1 medium green bell pepper, chopped

2 cloves garlic, minced

1 or 2 canned chipotle peppers in adobo sauce, finely chopped

1 cup water

1 can (6 ounces) tomato paste

2 cans (about 15 ounces) pinto or pink beans, drained and rinsed

1 can (about 15 ounces) small white beans, drained and rinsed

1 can (about 15 ounces) chickpeas

1 cup frozen or canned corn, drained and thawed

Salt

Sour cream (optional)

Shredded Cheddar cheese (optional)

Additional chopped onion (optional)

1. Heat oil in large nonstick skillet over medium heat. Add onion, bell pepper and garlic. Cook and stir until onion is translucent. Transfer to **CROCK-POT®** slow cooker.

2. Stir in chipotle peppers, water and tomato paste. Add pinto beans, white beans, chickpeas and corn. Cover; cook on LOW 3½ to 4 hours. Season to taste with salt. Garnish as desired.

Makes 8 servings

Nutrition Information

Calories	220
Total Fat	5g
Saturated Fat	1g
Protein	10g
Carbohydrate	35g
Cholesterol	0mg
Fiber	9g
Sodium	790mg

Dietary Exchanges:
1 Vegetable, 2 Starch, 1 Fat

Nutrition Information

Calories	122
Total Fat	3g
Saturated Fat	<1g
Protein	6g
Carbohydrate	20g
Cholesterol	9mg
Fiber	7g
Sodium	99mg

Dietary Exchanges:
1 Vegetable, 1 Starch, ½ Fat

Italian Eggplant with Millet and Pepper Stuffing

- ¼ cup uncooked millet
- 2 small eggplants (about ¾ pound total)
- ¼ cup chopped red bell pepper, divided
- ¼ cup chopped green bell pepper, divided
- 1 teaspoon olive oil
- 1 clove garlic, minced
- 1½ cups fat-free reduced-sodium vegetable broth
- ½ teaspoon ground cumin
- ½ teaspoon dried oregano
- ⅛ teaspoon red pepper flakes

1. Heat large heavy skillet over medium heat; cook and stir millet 5 minutes or until golden. Transfer to small bowl; set aside.

2. Cut eggplants lengthwise into halves. Scoop out flesh, leaving about ¼-inch-thick shell. Reserve shells; chop eggplant flesh. Combine 1 tablespoon red bell pepper and 1 teaspoon green bell pepper in small bowl; set aside.

3. Heat oil in skillet over medium heat. Add chopped eggplant, remaining red and green bell pepper and garlic; cook and stir about 8 minutes or until eggplant is tender.

4. Combine all ingredients except reserved eggplant shells and chopped bell peppers in **CROCK-POT®** slow cooker. Cover and cook on LOW 4½ hours or until all liquid is absorbed and millet is tender.

5. Fill eggplant shells with eggplant-millet mixture. Sprinkle with reserved chopped bell peppers, pressing in lightly. Turn **CROCK-POT®** slow cooker to HIGH. Carefully place filled shells in **CROCK-POT®** slow cooker. Cover and cook 1½ to 2 hours.

Makes 4 servings

Chunky Vegetable Chili

- **2 cans (about 15 ounces each) Great Northern beans, rinsed and drained**
- **1 cup frozen corn**
- **1 cup water**
- **1 onion, chopped**
- **2 stalks celery, diced**
- **1 carrot, diced**
- **1 can (6 ounces) tomato paste**
- **1 can (4 ounces) diced mild green chiles, undrained**
- **3 cloves garlic, minced**
- **1 tablespoon chili powder**
- **2 teaspoons dried oregano**
- **½ teaspoon salt**

Combine all ingredients in **CROCK-POT®** slow cooker. Cover; cook on LOW 5½ to 6 hours or until vegetables are tender.

Makes 6 servings

Nutrition Information

Calories	190
Total Fat	1g
Saturated Fat	0g
Protein	11g
Carbohydrate	35g
Cholesterol	0mg
Fiber	11g
Sodium	760mg

Dietary Exchanges:
2 Vegetable, 1½ Starch, ½ Meat

Nutrition Information

Calories	193
Total Fat	2g
Saturated Fat	<1g
Protein	6g
Carbohydrate	40g
Cholesterol	0mg
Fiber	6g
Sodium	194mg

Dietary Exchanges:
½ Vegetable, 2½ Starch

Quinoa & Vegetable Medley

Nonstick cooking spray

2 **medium sweet potatoes, cut into ½-inch-thick slices**

1 **medium eggplant, peeled and cut into ½-inch cubes**

1 **large green bell pepper, sliced**

1 **medium tomato, cut into wedges**

1 **small onion, cut into wedges**

½ **teaspoon salt**

¼ **teaspoon black pepper**

¼ **teaspoon ground red pepper**

1 **cup uncooked quinoa**

2 **cups water or fat-free reduced-sodium vegetable broth**

2 **cloves garlic, minced**

½ **teaspoon dried thyme**

¼ **teaspoon dried marjoram**

1. Coat **CROCK-POT®** slow cooker with nonstick cooking spray. Combine sweet potatoes, eggplant, bell pepper, tomato, onion, salt, black pepper and ground red pepper in **CROCK-POT®** slow cooker; mix well.

2. Meanwhile, place quinoa in strainer; rinse well. Add to vegetable mixture. Stir in water, garlic, thyme and marjoram. Cover; cook on LOW 5 hours or on HIGH 2½ hours until quinoa is tender and broth is absorbed.

Makes 6 servings

No-Fuss Macaroni & Cheese

- **2 cups (about 8 ounces) uncooked elbow macaroni**
- **3 ounces light pasteurized processed cheese, cubed**
- **1 cup (4 ounces) shredded reduced-fat mild Cheddar cheese**
- **½ teaspoon salt**
- **⅛ teaspoon black pepper**
- **1½ cups fat-free (skim) milk**

Combine macaroni, cheeses, salt and pepper in **CROCK-POT®** slow cooker; pour in milk. Cover; cook on LOW 2 to 3 hours, stirring after 20 minutes.

Makes 8 servings

Nutrition Information

Calories	190
Total Fat	5g
Saturated Fat	3g
Protein	11g
Carbohydrate	25g
Cholesterol	15mg
Fiber	1g
Sodium	470mg

Dietary Exchanges:
1½ Starch, 1 Meat, ½ Fat

Pasta, Potato, and Rice Sides

Slow Cooked Succotash

2 teaspoons canola oil

1 cup diced onion

1 cup diced green bell pepper

1 cup diced celery

1 teaspoon paprika

1½ cups frozen white or yellow corn

1½ cups frozen lima beans

1 cup canned low-sodium diced tomatoes, undrained

2 teaspoons dried parsley flakes *or* 1 tablespoon minced fresh parsley

½ teaspoon salt

½ teaspoon black pepper

1. Heat oil in large nonstick skillet over medium heat. Add onion, bell pepper and celery; cook and stir 5 minutes or until onion is translucent and pepper and celery are crisp-tender. Stir in paprika.

2. Combine onion, bell pepper and celery with remaining ingredients in **CROCK-POT®** slow cooker; mix well. Cover; cook on LOW 6 to 8 hours or on HIGH 3 to 4 hours.

Makes 8 servings

Nutrition Information

Calories	99
Total Fat	2g
Saturated Fat	<1g
Protein	4g
Carbohydrate	19g
Cholesterol	0mg
Fiber	4g
Sodium	187mg

Dietary Exchanges:
1 Starch, ½ Fat

Nutrition Information

Calories.............................146
Total Fat...............................2g
Saturated Fat.....................<1g
Protein 8g
Carbohydrate....................24g
Cholesterol.....................0mg
Fiber.....................................6g
Sodium..........................209mg

Dietary Exchanges:
1½ Starch, ½ Meat, ½ Fat

Confetti Black Beans

1	cup dried black beans
3	cups water
1½	teaspoons olive oil
1	medium onion, chopped
¼	cup chopped red bell pepper
¼	cup chopped yellow bell pepper
1	jalapeño pepper, finely chopped*
1	large tomato, seeded and chopped
½	teaspoon salt
⅛	teaspoon black pepper
2	cloves garlic, minced
1	can (about 14 ounces) reduced-sodium chicken broth
1	bay leaf
	Hot pepper sauce (optional)

*Jalapeño peppers can sting and irritate the skin, so wear rubber gloves when handling peppers and do not touch your eyes.

1. Sort and rinse beans; cover with water. Soak 8 hours or overnight. Drain.

2. Heat oil in large nonstick skillet over medium heat. Add onion, bell peppers and jalapeño pepper; cook and stir 5 minutes or until onion is tender. Add tomato, salt and black pepper; cook 5 minutes. Stir in garlic.

3. Place beans, broth and bay leaf in **CROCK-POT**® slow cooker. Add onion mixture; mix well. Cover; cook on LOW 7 to 8 hours or on HIGH 4½ to 5 hours or until beans are tender. Remove and discard bay leaf before serving. Serve with hot pepper sauce, if desired.

Makes 6 servings

Nutrition Information

Calories	230
Total Fat	6g
Saturated Fat	1g
Protein	5g
Carbohydrate	41g
Cholesterol	0mg
Fiber	4g
Sodium	770mg

Dietary Exchanges:
1½ Vegetable, 1½ Starch, 1 Fat

Tip

Jollof Rice (also spelled "jolof" or sometimes "djolof") is an important dish in many West African cultures.

Vegetable Jollof Rice

- **1 medium eggplant (about 1¼ pounds), trimmed and cut into 1-inch cubes**
- **1½ teaspoons salt, divided**
- **3 tablespoons vegetable oil, plus more as needed, divided**
- **1 medium onion, chopped**
- **1 medium green bell pepper, seeded and chopped**
- **3 medium carrots, cut into ½-inch-thick rounds**
- **2 cloves garlic, minced**
- **1½ cups converted rice**
- **1 tablespoon plus ½ teaspoon chili powder**
- **1 can (about 28 ounces) diced tomatoes in juice**
- **1 can (about 14 ounces) reduced-sodium vegetable broth**

1. Place eggplant cubes in colander. Toss with 1 teaspoon salt. Let stand 1 hour to drain. Rinse under cold water; drain and pat dry with paper towels.

2. Heat 1 tablespoon oil in large nonstick skillet over medium-high heat. Add eggplant to skillet in batches and cook, turning to brown on all sides. Remove eggplant to plate. Add additional oil, 1 tablespoon at a time, to skillet as needed.

3. Wipe out skillet with paper towels. Heat 1 tablespoon oil over medium-high heat. Add onion, bell pepper, carrots and garlic. Cook and stir about 10 minutes or until onion is soft but not brown. Transfer to **CROCK-POT®** slow cooker. Stir in rice, chili powder and remaining ½ teaspoon salt.

4. Drain tomatoes over 1-quart measuring cup, reserving juice. Add broth to juice; add additional water as needed to measure 4 cups. Pour into **CROCK-POT®** slow cooker. Stir in tomatoes; top with eggplant. Cover; cook on LOW 3½ to 4 hours or until rice is tender and liquid is absorbed.

Makes 8 servings

Nutrition Information

Calories	238
Total Fat	8g
Saturated Fat	1g
Protein	6g
Carbohydrate	37g
Cholesterol	1mg
Fiber	4g
Sodium	693mg

Dietary Exchanges:
1 Vegetable, 2 Starch, 1½ Fat

Mixed Grain Tabbouleh

3	cups canned chicken broth, divided
1	cup uncooked long-grain brown rice
½	cup uncooked bulgur wheat
1	cup chopped tomatoes
½	cup minced green onions
¼	cup chopped fresh mint leaves
¼	cup chopped fresh basil leaves
¼	cup chopped fresh oregano leaves
3	tablespoons fresh lemon juice
3	tablespoons olive oil
½	teaspoon salt
½	teaspoon black pepper

1. Combine broth, brown rice and bulgur in **CROCK-POT®** slow cooker. Cover; cook on LOW 7 hours or on HIGH 2½ to 3 hours until rice and bulgur are tender.

2. Combine remaining ingredients in large bowl. Stir in rice and bulgur; mix well. Cool completely before serving.

Makes 6 servings

Nutrition Information

Calories	320
Total Fat	8g
Saturated Fat	3g
Protein	7g
Carbohydrate	49g
Cholesterol	10mg
Fiber	2g
Sodium	690mg

Dietary Exchanges:
1/2 Vegetable, 2 1/2 Starch,
1 1/2 Fat

Spinach Risotto

- **2 teaspoons unsalted butter**
- **2 teaspoons olive oil**
- **3 tablespoons finely chopped shallot**
- **1 1/4 cups arborio rice**
- **1/2 cup dry white wine**
- **3 cups fat-free reduced-sodium chicken broth**
- **1/2 teaspoon salt**
- **2 cups baby spinach**
- **1/4 cup grated Parmesan cheese**
- **2 tablespoons pine nuts, toasted***

*To toast pine nuts, spread in single layer in heavy-bottomed skillet. Cook and stir over medium heat 1 to 2 minutes or until nuts are lightly browned. Remove from skillet immediately. Cool before using.

1. Melt butter in medium nonstick skillet over medium heat; add olive oil and shallot. Cook and stir until softened but not browned.

2. Stir in rice and cook 2 to 3 minutes or until chalky and well coated. Stir in wine and cook until reduced by approximately one half.

3. Transfer rice mixture to **CROCK-POT®** slow cooker. Add broth and salt; mix well. Cover; cook on HIGH 2 to 2 1/2 hours or until rice is almost cooked but still contains a little liquid.

4. Add spinach; mix well. Cover and cook 15 to 20 minutes or until spinach is cooked and rice is tender and creamy. Gently stir in cheese and pine nuts just before serving.

Makes 4 servings

Nutrition Information

Calories	118
Total Fat	3g
Saturated Fat	<1g
Protein	6g
Carbohydrate	20g
Cholesterol	0mg
Fiber	6g
Sodium	521mg

Dietary Exchanges:
1 Vegetable, 1 Starch, ½ Fat

Hot Three-Bean Casserole

- 2 **tablespoons olive oil**
- 1 **cup coarsely chopped onion**
- 1 **cup chopped celery**
- 2 **cloves garlic, minced**
- 2½ **cups (10 ounces) frozen cut green beans**
- 1 **can (about 15 ounces) chickpeas, rinsed and drained**
- 1 **can (about 15 ounces) kidney beans, rinsed and drained**
- 1 **cup coarsely chopped tomato**
- 1 **cup water**
- 1 **can (about 8 ounces) tomato sauce**
- 1 to 2 **jalapeño peppers, minced***
- 1 **tablespoon chili powder**
- 2 **teaspoons sugar**
- 1½ **teaspoons ground cumin**
- 1 **teaspoon salt**
- 1 **teaspoon dried oregano**
- ¼ **teaspoon black pepper**
- **Fresh oregano (optional)**

Jalapeño peppers can sting and irritate the skin, so wear rubber gloves when handling peppers and do not touch your eyes.

1. Heat oil in large nonstick skillet over medium heat. Add onion, celery and garlic; cook and stir 5 minutes or until tender. Transfer to **CROCK-POT®** slow cooker.

2. Add all remaining ingredients except fresh oregano to **CROCK-POT®** slow cooker; mix well. Cover and cook on LOW 6 to 8 hours. Garnish with fresh oregano.

Makes 12 servings

Nutrition Information

Calories	150
Total Fat	5g
Saturated Fat	3g
Protein	5g
Carbohydrate	23g
Cholesterol	10mg
Fiber	3g
Sodium	270mg

Dietary Exchanges:
1 Starch, 1 Fat

Escalloped Corn

2 tablespoons unsalted butter

½ cup chopped onion

3 tablespoons all-purpose flour

1 cup fat-free (skim) milk

4 cups frozen corn, thawed, divided

½ teaspoon salt

½ teaspoon dried thyme

¼ teaspoon black pepper

⅛ teaspoon ground nutmeg

Fresh thyme (optional)

1. Melt butter in small saucepan over medium heat. Add onion; cook and stir 5 minutes or until tender. Add flour; cook over medium heat 1 minute, stirring constantly. Stir in milk; bring to a boil. Boil 1 minute or until thickened, stirring constantly.

2. Process 2 cups corn in food processor or blender until coarsely chopped. Combine milk mixture, chopped corn and remaining 2 cups whole corn, salt, dried thyme, pepper and nutmeg in **CROCK-POT®** slow cooker; mix well. Cover; cook on LOW 3½ to 4 hours or until mixture is bubbly around edge. Garnish with fresh thyme.

Makes 6 servings

Nutrition Information

Calories	250
Total Fat	8g
Saturated Fat	3g
Protein	5g
Carbohydrate	43g
Cholesterol	60mg
Fiber	3g
Sodium	240mg

Dietary Exchanges:
1½ Starch, 1½ Fat, ½ Other

Sweet Potato & Pecan Casserole

1 can (40 ounces) sweet potatoes, drained and mashed
½ cup apple juice
4 tablespoons unsalted butter, melted, divided
½ teaspoon salt
½ teaspoon ground cinnamon
¼ teaspoon black pepper
2 eggs, beaten
⅓ cup brown sugar
¼ cup chopped pecans
2 tablespoons all-purpose flour

1. Combine sweet potatoes, apple juice, 2 tablespoons butter, salt, cinnamon and pepper in large bowl. Beat in eggs. Transfer mixture to **CROCK-POT®** slow cooker.

2. Combine brown sugar, pecans, flour and remaining 2 tablespoons butter in small bowl. Spread over sweet potatoes in **CROCK-POT®** slow cooker. Cover; cook on HIGH 3 to 4 hours.

Makes 8 servings

Pasta, Potato, and Rice Sides

Candied Sweet Potatoes

Nutrition Information

Calories	183
Total Fat	10g
Saturated Fat	1g
Protein	2g
Carbohydrate	21g
Cholesterol	35mg
Fiber	<1g
Sodium	129mg

Dietary Exchanges:
1½ Starch, 2 Fat

3   **medium sweet potatoes (1½ to 2 pounds), peeled and sliced into ½-inch rounds**

¼   **cup (½ stick) margarine, cut into pieces**

10   **packets sugar substitute**

½   **cup water**

1   **tablespoon vanilla**

1   **teaspoon nutmeg**

Combine all ingredients in **CROCK-POT**® slow cooker; mix well. Cover; cook on LOW 7 hours or on HIGH 4 hours or until potatoes are tender.

Makes 4 servings

Mashed Rutabagas and Potatoes

Nutrition Information

Calories	93
Total Fat	1g
Saturated Fat	<1g
Protein	3g
Carbohydrate	20g
Cholesterol	1mg
Fiber	3g
Sodium	30mg

Dietary Exchanges:
2 Vegetable, ½ Starch

2   **pounds rutabagas, peeled, cut into ½-inch pieces**

1   **pound potatoes, peeled, cut into ½-inch pieces**

½   **cup low-fat (1%) milk**

½   **teaspoon ground nutmeg**

2   **tablespoons chopped fresh parsley**

1. Combine rutabagas and potatoes in **CROCK-POT**® slow cooker; add enough water to cover. Cover; cook on LOW 6 hours or on HIGH 3 hours or until tender.

2. Using a slotted spoon, transfer vegetables to large bowl. Discard cooking liquid. Mash vegetables with potato masher. Heat milk in small saucepan over medium heat or place in microwavable bowl and microwave on HIGH 5 minutes or until warm. Add milk and nutmeg to vegetables; mix well. Stir in parsley before serving.

Makes 8 servings

Candied Sweet Potatoes

Nutrition Information

Calories	130
Total Fat	1g
Saturated Fat	0g
Protein	2g
Carbohydrate	30g
Cholesterol	0mg
Fiber	4g
Sodium	10mg

Dietary Exchanges:
3½ Vegetable, 1½ Starch

Cran-Orange Acorn Squash

- **3** small acorn or carnival squash
- **5** tablespoons instant brown rice
- **3** tablespoons minced onion
- **3** tablespoons diced celery
- **3** tablespoons dried cranberries
   Pinch ground or dried sage
- **1** teaspoon unsalted butter, cut into bits
- **3** tablespoons orange juice
- **½** cup warm water

1. Slice off tops of squash and enough of bottoms so squash will sit upright. Scoop out seeds and discard; set squash aside.

2. Combine rice, onion, celery, cranberries and sage in small bowl. Stuff each squash with rice mixture; dot with butter. Pour 1 tablespoon orange juice into each squash over stuffing.

3. Stand squash in **CROCK-POT®** slow cooker. Pour water into bottom of **CROCK-POT®** slow cooker. Cover; cook on LOW 2½ hours or until squash are tender.

Makes 6 servings

Mediterranean Red Potatoes

- **3** **medium red potatoes, cut into bite-size pieces**
- **⅔** **cup fresh or frozen pearl onions**
  Nonstick cooking spray
- **¾** **teaspoon dried Italian seasoning**
- **¼** **teaspoon black pepper**
- **1** **small tomato, seeded and chopped**
- **2** **ounces (½ cup) feta cheese, crumbled**
- **2** **tablespoons chopped black olives**

1. Place potatoes and onions in 1½-quart soufflé dish. Spray with nonstick cooking spray; toss to coat. Add Italian seasoning and pepper; mix well. Cover dish tightly with foil.

2. Tear off three 18×3-inch strips of heavy-duty foil. Cross strips to resemble wheel spokes. Place soufflé dish in center of strips. Pull foil strips up and over dish to create handles and place dish into **CROCK-POT®** slow cooker.

3. Pour hot water into **CROCK-POT®** slow cooker to about 1½ inches from top of soufflé dish. Cover; cook on LOW 7 to 8 hours.

4. Use foil handles to lift dish out of **CROCK-POT®** slow cooker. Add tomato, cheese and olives to potato mixture; mix well.

Makes 4 servings

Nutrition Information

Calories	158
Total Fat	8g
Saturated Fat	3g
Protein	4g
Carbohydrate	20g
Cholesterol	13mg
Fiber	2g
Sodium	335mg

Dietary Exchanges:
1 Vegetable, 1 Starch, 1½ Fat

Nutrition Information

Calories...............................200
Total Fat.............................8g
Saturated Fat........................1g
Protein 3g
Carbohydrate...................28g
Cholesterol......................5mg
Fiber.....................................3g
Sodium...........................150mg

Dietary Exchanges:
2 Starch, 1½ Fat

Chunky Ranch Potatoes

3 pounds medium red potatoes, unpeeled and quartered

1 cup water

½ cup prepared ranch dressing

½ cup grated Parmesan or Cheddar cheese (optional)

¼ cup minced chives

1. Place potatoes in **CROCK-POT®** slow cooker. Add water. Cover; cook on LOW 7 to 9 hours or on HIGH 4 to 6 hours or until potatoes are tender.

2. Stir in ranch dressing, cheese, if desired, and chives. Use spoon to break potatoes into chunks. Serve hot or cold.

Makes 8 servings

Supper Squash Medley

2 **butternut squash, peeled, seeded and diced (about 4 cups)**

1 **can (28 ounces) tomatoes, undrained**

1 **can (15 ounces) corn, drained**

2 **medium onions, chopped**

2 **medium green bell peppers, chopped**

2 **teaspoons minced garlic**

2 **green chiles, chopped**

1 **cup fat-free chicken broth**

1 **teaspoon salt**

½ **teaspoon black pepper**

1 **can (6 ounces) tomato paste**

1. Combine squash, tomatoes with juice, corn, onions, bell peppers, garlic, chiles, broth, salt and black pepper in **CROCK-POT®** slow cooker. Cover; cook on LOW 6 hours.

2. Remove about ½ cup cooking liquid and blend with tomato paste. Add back to **CROCK-POT®** slow cooker and stir well. Cook 30 minutes or until mixture is slightly thickened and heated through.

Makes 8 to 10 servings

Nutrition Information	
Calories	150
Total Fat	1g
Saturated Fat	0g
Protein	5g
Carbohydrate	32g
Cholesterol	0mg
Fiber	5g
Sodium	650mg

Dietary Exchanges:
3½ Vegetable, 2 Starch

Nutrition Information

Calories	150
Total Fat	5g
Saturated Fat	3g
Protein	7g
Carbohydrate	19g
Cholesterol	15mg
Fiber	1g
Sodium	800mg

Dietary Exchanges:
1 Starch, ½ Meat

Polenta-Style Corn Casserole

1 **can (about 14 ounces) fat-free chicken broth**

½ **cup cornmeal**

1 **can (7 ounces) corn, drained**

1 **can (4 ounces) diced green chiles, drained**

¼ **cup diced red bell pepper**

½ **teaspoon salt**

¼ **teaspoon black pepper**

1 **cup (4 ounces) shredded reduced-fat Cheddar cheese**

1. Pour broth into **CROCK-POT**® slow cooker. Whisk in cornmeal. Add corn, chiles, bell pepper, salt and black pepper. Cover; cook on LOW 4 to 5 hours or on HIGH 2 to 3 hours.

2. Stir in cheese. Cook, uncovered, 15 to 30 minutes or until cheese is melted.

Makes 6 servings

Mushroom Wild Rice

1	**cup uncooked wild rice**
½	**cup sliced mushrooms**
½	**cup diced onion**
½	**cup diced green or red bell pepper**
1½	**cups fat-free reduced-sodium chicken broth**
1	**tablespoon olive oil**
¼	**teaspoon salt**
¼	**teaspoon black pepper**

Layer rice, mushrooms, onion and bell pepper in **CROCK-POT®** slow cooker. Add broth, oil, salt and pepper. Cover; cook on HIGH 2½ hours or until rice is tender and liquid is absorbed.

Makes 8 servings

Nutrition Information

Calories	100
Total Fat	2g
Saturated Fat	<1g
Protein	4g
Carbohydrate	17g
Cholesterol	5mg
Fiber	2g
Sodium	148mg

Dietary Exchanges:
1 Starch, ½ Fat

Nutrition Information

Calories	190
Total Fat	8g
Saturated Fat	3g
Protein	5g
Carbohydrate	25g
Cholesterol	60mg
Fiber	1g
Sodium	610mg

Dietary Exchanges:
1 Starch, 1 Fat

Mexican Corn Bread Pudding

Nonstick cooking spray

1 **can (14¾ ounces) cream-style corn**

¾ **cup yellow cornmeal**

2 **eggs, beaten**

1 **can (4 ounces) diced mild green chiles**

2 **tablespoons vegetable oil**

2 **tablespoons sugar**

2 **teaspoons baking powder**

¾ **teaspoon salt**

½ **cup shredded Cheddar cheese**

1. Coat 2-quart **CROCK-POT®** slow cooker with nonstick cooking spray. Combine corn, cornmeal, eggs, chiles, oil, sugar, baking powder and salt in medium bowl; mix well. Pour into **CROCK-POT®** slow cooker. Cover; cook on LOW 2 to 2½ hours or until center is set.

2. Top with cheese. Cover and let stand 5 minutes or until cheese is melted.

Makes 8 servings

Lemon-Mint Red Potatoes

Nonstick cooking spray

2 **pounds new red potatoes**

3 **tablespoons extra-virgin olive oil**

1 **teaspoon salt**

¾ **teaspoon dried Greek seasoning or dried oregano**

¼ **teaspoon garlic powder**

¼ **teaspoon black pepper**

¼ **cup chopped fresh mint leaves, divided**

2 **tablespoons lemon juice**

1 **teaspoon grated lemon peel**

1 **tablespoon unsalted butter**

1. Coat **CROCK-POT®** slow cooker with nonstick cooking spray. Add potatoes and oil, stirring gently to coat. Sprinkle with salt, Greek seasoning, garlic powder and pepper. Cover and cook on LOW 7 hours or on HIGH 4 hours.

2. Turn **CROCK-POT®** slow cooker to HIGH. Add 2 tablespoons mint, lemon juice, lemon peel and butter; stir until butter is completely melted. Cover; cook 15 minutes. Garnish with remaining 2 tablespoons mint.

Makes 6 servings

Nutrition Information

Calories	190
Total Fat	9g
Saturated Fat	2g
Protein	3g
Carbohydrate	25g
Cholesterol	5mg
Fiber	3g
Sodium	400mg

Dietary Exchanges:
1½ Starch, 2 Fat

Tip

It's easy to prepare these potatoes ahead of time. Simply follow the recipe and then turn off the heat. Let it stand at room temperature for up to 2 hours. You may reheat or serve the potatoes at room temperature.

Nutrition Information

Calories.................................190
Total Fat................................5g
Saturated Fat.......................3g
Protein 5g
Carbohydrate.....................31g
Cholesterol.....................15mg
Fiber.......................................4g
Sodium..........................610mg

Dietary Exchanges:
1 Fat, 2 Starch

Rustic Garlic Mashed Potatoes

2 pounds baking potatoes, unpeeled and cut into ½-inch cubes

¼ **cup water**

2 tablespoons unsalted butter, cut into ⅛-inch pieces

1¼ **teaspoons salt**

½ **teaspoon garlic powder**

¼ **teaspoon black pepper**

1 cup fat-free (skim) milk

1. Combine all ingredients except milk in **CROCK-POT**® slow cooker; mix well. Cover; cook on LOW 7 hours or on HIGH 4 hours.

2. Add milk to potatoes; mash with potato masher until smooth.

Makes 5 servings

Barley & Vegetable Risotto

- **2 teaspoons olive oil**
- **1 small onion, diced**
- **8 ounces sliced mushrooms**
- **¾ cup uncooked pearl barley**
- **1 large red bell pepper, diced**
- **4½ cups fat-free reduced-sodium vegetable or chicken broth**
- **2 cups packed baby spinach**
- **¼ cup grated Parmesan cheese**
- **¼ teaspoon black pepper**

1. Heat olive oil in large nonstick skillet over medium-high heat. Add onion, cook and stir 2 minutes or until lightly browned. Add mushrooms; cook and stir 5 minutes or until mushrooms begin to brown. Transfer to **CROCK-POT®** slow cooker.

2. Add barley and bell pepper; pour in broth. Cover; cook on LOW 4 to 5 hours or on HIGH 2½ to 3 hours or until barley is tender and liquid is absorbed.

3. Add spinach; mix well. Let stand 5 minutes. Gently stir in cheese and black pepper just before serving.

Makes 6 servings

Nutrition Information

Calories	70
Total Fat	3g
Saturated Fat	1g
Protein	3g
Carbohydrate	7g
Cholesterol	5mg
Fiber	2g
Sodium	340mg

Dietary Exchanges:
1 Vegetable, ½ Fat

Vegetable Sides

Sunshine Squash

1 butternut squash (about 2 pounds) peeled, seeded and diced

1 can (15 ounces) corn, drained

1 can (about 14 ounces) diced tomatoes, undrained

1 medium onion, coarsely chopped

1 medium green bell pepper, cut into 1-inch pieces

½ cup fat-free reduced-sodium chicken broth

1 green chile pepper, coarsely chopped

1 clove garlic, minced

½ teaspoon salt

¼ teaspoon black pepper

1 tablespoon plus 1½ teaspoons tomato paste

1. Combine all ingredients except tomato paste in **CROCK-POT**® slow cooker; mix well. Cover; cook on LOW 6 hours or until squash is tender.

2. Remove about ¼ cup cooking liquid and blend with tomato paste. Stir into **CROCK-POT**® slow cooker. Cook 30 minutes or until mixture is slightly thickened and heated through.

Makes 6 to 8 servings

Nutrition Information

Calories	170
Total Fat	1g
Saturated Fat	0g
Protein	5g
Carbohydrate	39g
Cholesterol	0mg
Fiber	5g
Sodium	640mg

Dietary Exchanges:
4 Vegetable, 3½ Starch

221

Nutrition Information

Calories	120
Total Fat	6g
Saturated Fat	0g
Protein	2g
Carbohydrate	16g
Cholesterol	0mg
Fiber	5g
Sodium	380mg

Dietary Exchanges:
2 Vegetable, 1 Fat

Eggplant Italiano

- 1¼ **pounds eggplant, cut into 1-inch cubes**
- 2 **medium onions, thinly sliced**
- 2 **medium stalks celery, cut into 1-inch pieces**
- 1 **can (about 16 ounces) diced tomatoes**
- 3 **tablespoons tomato sauce**
- 1 **tablespoon olive oil, divided**
- ½ **cup pitted ripe olives, halved**
- 2 **tablespoons balsamic vinegar**
- 1 **tablespoon sugar**
- 1 **tablespoon capers, drained**
- 1 **teaspoon dried oregano or basil**
  Salt and black pepper to taste
  Fresh basil leaves, leaf lettuce and jalapeño pepper* (optional)

*Jalapeño peppers can sting and irritate the skin, so wear rubber gloves when handling peppers and do not touch your eyes.

1. Combine eggplant, onions, celery, tomatoes, tomato sauce and oil in **CROCK-POT®** slow cooker; mix well. Cover; cook on LOW 3½ to 4 hours or until eggplant is tender.

2. Add olives, vinegar, sugar, capers and oregano to **CROCK-POT®** slow cooker; mix well. Season with salt and pepper. Cover and cook 45 minutes to 1 hour or until heated through. Garnish as desired.

Makes 6 servings

Nutrition Information

Calories	60
Total Fat	0g
Saturated Fat	0g
Protein	1g
Carbohydrate	10g
Cholesterol	0mg
Fiber	2g
Sodium	520mg

Dietary Exchanges:
2 Vegetable

Tarragon Carrots in White Wine

½ **cup fat-free chicken broth**

½ **cup dry white wine**

1 **tablespoon lemon juice**

1 **tablespoon minced fresh tarragon**

2 **teaspoons finely chopped green onions**

1½ **teaspoons chopped flat-leaf parsley**

1 **clove garlic, minced**

1 **teaspoon salt**

8 **medium carrots, peeled and cut into matchsticks**

2 **tablespoons melba toast, crushed**

2 **tablespoons cold water**

1. Combine broth, wine, lemon juice, tarragon, onions, parsley, garlic and salt in **CROCK-POT®** slow cooker. Add carrots; stir well to combine. Cover; cook on LOW 2½ to 3 hours or on HIGH 1½ to 2 hours.

2. Turn **CROCK-POT®** slow cooker to LOW. Dissolve toast crumbs in water and add to carrots. Cover; cook 10 minutes longer or until thickened.

Makes 6 to 8 servings

Nutrition Information

Calories	150
Total Fat	12g
Saturated Fat	3g
Protein	4g
Carbohydrate	8g
Cholesterol	5mg
Fiber	2g
Sodium	370mg

Dietary Exchanges:
1½ Vegetable, 2 Fat

Roasted Summer Squash with Pine Nuts and Romano Cheese

- **2 tablespoons extra-virgin olive oil**
- **½ cup chopped yellow onion**
- **1 medium red bell pepper, cored, seeded and chopped**
- **1 clove garlic, minced**
- **3 medium zucchini, cut in ½-inch slices**
- **3 medium summer squash, cut in ½-inch slices**
- **½ cup chopped pine nuts**
- **⅓ cup grated Romano cheese**
- **1 teaspoon dried Italian seasoning**
- **1 teaspoon salt**
- **¼ teaspoon black pepper**
- **1 tablespoon unsalted butter, cut into small cubes**

1. Heat oil in skillet over medium-high heat until hot. Add onion, bell pepper and garlic. Cook and stir until onions are translucent and soft, about 10 minutes. Transfer to **CROCK-POT®** slow cooker.

2. Add zucchini and summer squash. Toss lightly.

3. Combine pine nuts, cheese, Italian seasoning, salt and pepper in small bowl. Fold half of cheese mixture into squash. Sprinkle remaining cheese mixture on top. Dot cheese with butter. Cover; cook on LOW 4 to 6 hours.

Makes 8 servings

Nutrition Information

Calories.................................125
Total Fat....................................1g
Saturated Fat....................<1g
Protein 15g
Carbohydrate....................13g
Cholesterol.......................6mg
Fiber...5g
Sodium..........................537mg

Dietary Exchanges:
1 Vegetable, 2 Meat

Spinach Artichoke Gratin

- **2 cups (16 ounces) fat-free cottage cheese**
- **½ cup cholesterol-free egg substitute**
- **4½ tablespoons grated Parmesan cheese, divided**
- **1 tablespoon lemon juice**
- **⅛ teaspoon black pepper**
- **⅛ teaspoon ground nutmeg**
- **Nonstick cooking spray**
- **2 packages (10 ounces each) frozen chopped spinach, thawed**
- **⅓ cup thinly sliced green onions**
- **1 package (10 ounces) frozen artichoke hearts, thawed and halved**

1. Combine cottage cheese, egg substitute, 3 tablespoons Parmesan cheese, lemon juice, pepper and nutmeg in food processor; process until smooth.

2. Coat **CROCK-POT®** slow cooker with nonstick cooking spray. Squeeze moisture from spinach. Combine spinach, cottage cheese mixture and green onions in large bowl. Spread half of mixture in **CROCK-POT®** slow cooker.

3. Pat artichokes dry with paper towels. Place in single layer over spinach mixture. Sprinkle with remaining 1½ tablespoons Parmesan cheese. Cover with remaining spinach mixture. Cover; cook on LOW 3 to 3½ hours or on HIGH 2 to 2½ hours with lid slightly ajar to allow excess moisture to escape.

Makes 6 servings

Vegetable Sides

Nutrition Information

Calories.................................42
Total Fat...............................3g
Saturated Fat.......................0g
Protein ....<1g
Carbohydrate.......................4g
Cholesterol.....................0mg
Fiber.................................<1g
Sodium..........................141mg

Dietary Exchanges:
1 Vegetable, ½ Fat

Caponata

1 medium eggplant (about 1 pound), peeled and cut into ½-inch pieces

1 can (about 14 ounces) diced tomatoes

1 medium onion, chopped

1 red bell pepper, cut into ½-inch pieces

½ cup medium-hot salsa

¼ cup extra virgin olive oil

3 cloves garlic, minced

2 tablespoons capers, drained

2 tablespoons balsamic vinegar

1 teaspoon dried oregano

¼ teaspoon salt

⅓ cup packed fresh basil, cut into thin strips

Toasted sliced Italian or French bread

1. Combine eggplant, tomatoes, onion, bell pepper, salsa, oil, garlic, capers, vinegar, oregano and salt in **CROCK-POT®** slow cooker; mix well. Cover; cook on LOW 7 to 8 hours or until vegetables are crisp-tender.

2. Stir in basil. Serve at room temperature with toasted bread.

Makes about 5¼ cups

Nutrition Information

Calories	116
Total Fat	2g
Saturated Fat	<1g
Protein	4g
Carbohydrate	21g
Cholesterol	6mg
Fiber	6g
Sodium	253mg

Dietary Exchanges:
$3\frac{1}{2}$ Vegetable, $\frac{1}{2}$ Fat

Beets in Spicy Mustard Sauce

3 **pounds beets, peeled, halved, and cut into ½-inch slices**

5 **cups water**

¼ **cup reduced-fat sour cream**

2 **tablespoons spicy brown mustard**

2 **teaspoons lemon juice**

2 **cloves garlic, minced**

¼ **teaspoon black pepper**

⅛ **teaspoon dried thyme**

1. Place beets in **CROCK-POT®** slow cooker. Add enough water to cover by 1 inch. Cover and cook on LOW 7 to 8 hours or until beets are tender.

2. Combine sour cream, mustard, lemon juice, garlic, pepper and thyme in small bowl; spoon over beets, tossing gently to coat. Cover; cook 15 minutes.

Makes 4 servings

Nutrition Information

Calories	76
Total Fat	3g
Saturated Fat	<1g
Protein	2g
Carbohydrate	12g
Cholesterol	0mg
Fiber	4g
Sodium	194mg

Dietary Exchanges:
2 Vegetable, ½ Fat

Fennel Braised with Tomato

2 **bulbs fennel**

1 **tablespoon extra virgin olive oil**

1 **small onion, sliced**

1 **clove garlic, sliced**

4 **medium tomatoes, chopped**

⅔ **cup reduced-sodium vegetable broth or water**

3 **tablespoons dry white wine or vegetable broth**

1 **tablespoon chopped fresh marjoram *or* 1 teaspoon dried marjoram**

¼ **teaspoon salt**

¼ **teaspoon black pepper**

1. Trim stems and bottoms from fennel bulbs, reserving green leafy tops for garnish. Cut each bulb lengthwise into 4 wedges.

2. Heat oil in large nonstick skillet over medium heat. Cook and stir fennel, onion and garlic 5 minutes or until onion is translucent. Transfer to **CROCK-POT®** slow cooker.

3. Add all remaining ingredients to **CROCK-POT®** slow cooker; mix well. Cover; cook on LOW 2 to 3 hours or on HIGH 1 to 1½ hours or until vegetables are tender, stirring occasionally to ensure even cooking. Garnish with fennel leaves.

Makes 6 servings

Nutrition Information

Calories	72
Total Fat	2g
Saturated Fat	<1g
Protein	6g
Carbohydrate	11g
Cholesterol	0mg
Fiber	5g
Sodium	42mg

Dietary Exchanges:
2½ Vegetable

Garlicky Mustard Greens

2 pounds mustard greens

1 teaspoon olive oil

1 cup chopped onion

2 cloves garlic, minced

¾ cup chopped red bell pepper

½ cup fat-free reduced-sodium chicken or vegetable broth

1 tablespoons cider vinegar

1 teaspoons sugar

1. Remove stems and any wilted leaves from greens. Stack several leaves, roll up, and cut crosswise into 1-inch slices; repeat with remaining greens.

2. Heat oil in large saucepan over medium heat. Add onion and garlic; cook and stir 5 minutes or until onion is tender.

3. Combine all ingredients but vinegar and sugar in **CROCK-POT®** slow cooker. Cover; cook on LOW 3 to 4 hours or on HIGH 2 hours.

4. Combine vinegar and sugar in small bowl; stir until sugar is dissolved. Add to cooked greens; mix well. Serve immediately.

Makes 4 servings

Brussels Sprouts with Bacon, Thyme and Raisins

Nutrition Information

Calories	109
Total Fat	2g
Saturated Fat	<1g
Protein	6g
Carbohydrate	21g
Cholesterol	3mg
Fiber	5g
Sodium	110mg

Dietary Exchanges:
1 Vegetable, 1 Starch

- **2 pounds Brussels sprouts**
- **1 cup reduced-sodium chicken broth**
- **⅔ cup golden raisins**
- **2 thick slices applewood smoked bacon, chopped**
- **2 tablespoons chopped fresh thyme**

Trim ends from sprouts; cut in half lengthwise through core (or in quarters if large). Combine all ingredients in **CROCK-POT®** slow cooker. Cover; cook on LOW 3 to 4 hours.

Makes 8 servings

Collard Greens

Nutrition Information

Calories	64
Total Fat	5g
Saturated Fat	<1g
Protein	7g
Carbohydrate	6g
Cholesterol	0mg
Fiber	2g
Sodium	14mg

Dietary Exchanges:
1 Vegetable, 1 Fat

- **4 bunches collard greens, stemmed, torn into bite-size pieces**
- **2 cups water**
- **½ medium red bell pepper, cut into strips**
- **⅓ medium green bell pepper, cut into strips**
- **¼ cup olive oil**
- **¼ teaspoon salt**
- **¼ teaspoon black pepper**

Combine all ingredients in **CROCK-POT®** slow cooker. Cover; cook on LOW 3 to 4 hours or on HIGH 2 hours.

Makes 10 servings

Brussels Sprouts with
Bacon, Thyme and Raisins

Nutrition Information

Calories...............................144
Total Fat................................3g
Saturated Fat........................1g
Protein 2g
Carbohydrate.....................31g
Cholesterol......................0mg
Fiber....................................5g
Sodium..........................49mg

Dietary Exchanges:
1 Vegetable, 1½ Fruit, ½ Fat

Apple & Carrot Casserole

- **6 large carrots, peeled and sliced into ½-inch slices**
- **4 large apples, peeled, cored and sliced**
- **¼ cup plus 1 tablespoon all-purpose flour**
- **1 tablespoon packed brown sugar**
- **½ teaspoon ground nutmeg**
- **1 tablespoon butter**
- **½ cup orange juice**
- **½ teaspoon salt (optional)**

Layer carrots and apples in **CROCK-POT®** slow cooker. Combine flour, brown sugar and nutmeg in small bowl; sprinkle over top of carrots and apples. Dot with butter. Pour orange juice over flour mixture; sprinkle with salt, if desired. Cover; cook on LOW 3½ to 4 hours or until carrots are crisp-tender.

Makes 6 servings

Sweet-Sour Cabbage with Apples and Caraway Seeds

- **4 cups shredded red cabbage**
- **1 large tart apple, peeled, cored and cut crosswise into ¼-inch-thick slices**
- **¼ cup packed light brown sugar**
- **¼ cup water**
- **¼ cup cider vinegar**
- **½ teaspoon salt**
- **¼ teaspoon caraway seeds**
- **Dash black pepper**

Combine all ingredients in **CROCK-POT®** slow cooker. Cover; cook on LOW 2½ to 3 hours.

Makes 6 servings

Nutrition Information

Calories	62
Total Fat	<1g
Saturated Fat	<1g
Protein	1g
Carbohydrate	16g
Cholesterol	0mg
Fiber	2g
Sodium	191mg

Dietary Exchanges:
1 Vegetable, ½ Fruit

241

Nutrition Information

Calories.....................................54

Total Fat...................................2g

Saturated Fat.........................1g

Protein 3g

Carbohydrate.......................7g

Cholesterol........................6mg

Fiber..3g

Sodium.............................41mg

Dietary Exchanges:

1½ Vegetable, ½ Fat

Cauliflower Mash

2 heads cauliflower (about 8 cups florets)

1 tablespoon butter or as needed

1 tablespoon half-and-half, cream, whole milk, buttermilk, chicken broth, or as needed

Salt

1. Break cauliflower into equal-size florets. Arrange cauliflower in **CROCK-POT®** slow cooker and add enough water to fill **CROCK-POT®** about 2 inches. Cover; cook on LOW for 5 to 6 hours. Drain well.

2. Place cooked cauliflower in food processor or blender; process until almost smooth. Add butter; process until smooth, adding half-and-half as needed to reach desired consistency. Season with salt.

Makes 6 servings

Simmered Napa Cabbage with Dried Apricots

4 cups Napa cabbage or green cabbage, cored, cleaned and sliced thin

1 cup chopped dried apricots

¼ cup clover honey

2 tablespoons orange juice

½ cup dry red wine

Salt and black pepper, to taste

Grated orange peel (optional)

1. Combine cabbage and apricots in **CROCK-POT®** slow cooker. Toss to mix well.

2. Combine honey and orange juice, mixing until smooth. Drizzle over cabbage. Add wine. Cover; cook on LOW 5 to 6 hours or on HIGH 2 to 3 hours, or until cabbage is tender.

3. Season with salt and pepper. Garnish with orange peel.

Makes 8 servings

Nutrition Information	
Calories	130
Total Fat	0g
Saturated Fat	0g
Protein	2g
Carbohydrate	27g
Cholesterol	0mg
Fiber	2g
Sodium	10mg

Dietary Exchanges:
1½ Vegetable, 1 Fruit, ½ Other

Nutrition Information

Calories	42
Total Fat	<1g
Saturated Fat	<1g
Protein	1g
Carbohydrate	10g
Cholesterol	0mg
Fiber	2g
Sodium	118mg

Dietary Exchanges:
1 Vegetable, ½ Fruit

French Carrot Medley

2 **cups fresh or frozen sliced carrots**

¾ **cup unsweetened orange juice**

1 **can (4 ounces) sliced mushrooms, undrained**

4 **stalks celery, sliced**

2 **tablespoons chopped onion**

½ **teaspoon dill weed**

   Salt and black pepper to taste (optional)

¼ **cup cold water**

2 **teaspoons cornstarch**

1. Combine all ingredients except cornstarch and water in **CROCK-POT®** slow cooker. Cover; cook on LOW 3 to 4 hours or on HIGH 2 hours.

2. Whisk water into cornstarch in small bowl. Stir into cooking liquid in **CROCK-POT®** slow cooker and cook 15 minutes or until sauce is thickened. Spoon over carrots.

Makes 6 servings

Creamy Curried Spinach

3 packages (10 ounces each) frozen spinach, thawed

1 onion, chopped

4 teaspoons minced garlic

2 tablespoons curry powder

1 tablespoon unsalted butter, melted

¼ cup fat-free chicken broth

¼ cup light whipping cream

1 teaspoon lemon juice

Combine spinach, onion, garlic, curry powder, butter and broth in **CROCK-POT®** slow cooker. Cover; cook on LOW 3 to 4 hours or on HIGH 2 hours or until done. Stir in cream and lemon juice 30 minutes before end of cooking time.

Makes 8 servings

Nutrition Information

Calories..................................80

Total Fat................................5g

Saturated Fat.......................3g

Protein..................................4g

Carbohydrate......................7g

Cholesterol....................10mg

Fiber......................................4g

Sodium..........................110mg

Dietary Exchanges:
1 Vegetable, 1 Fat

Nutrition Information

Calories	53
Total Fat	2g
Saturated Fat	1g
Protein	4g
Carbohydrate	6g
Cholesterol	3mg
Fiber	3g
Sodium	116mg

Dietary Exchanges:
1 Vegetable, ½ Fat

Light Lemon Cauliflower

- **1 tablespoon reduced-fat margarine**
- **3 cloves garlic, minced**
- **½ cup water**
- **2 tablespoons fresh lemon juice**
- **6 cups (about 1½ pounds) cauliflower florets**
- **4 tablespoons chopped fresh parsley, divided**
- **½ teaspoon grated lemon peel**
- **¼ cup grated Parmesan cheese**
- **Lemon slices (optional)**

1. Heat margarine in small saucepan over medium heat. Add garlic; cook and stir 2 to 3 minutes or until soft. Stir in water and lemon juice. Transfer to **CROCK-POT®** slow cooker.

2. Add cauliflower, 1 tablespoon parsley and lemon peel to **CROCK-POT®** slow cooker; mix well. Cover; cook on LOW 4 hours.

3. Sprinkle with remaining 3 tablespoons parsley and cheese before serving. Garnish with lemon slices.

Makes 6 servings

Red Cabbage with Apples

1 **head red cabbage, shredded**

2 **apples, peeled and thinly sliced**

½ **cup sliced onion**

½ **cup unsweetened apple juice**

¼ **cup lemon juice**

2 **tablespoons raisins**

2 **tablespoons packed brown sugar**

Salt and black pepper (optional)

Combine all ingredients in **CROCK-POT®** slow cooker. Cover; cook on LOW 2½ to 3 hours. Season with salt and pepper, if desired.

Makes 8 servings

Nutrition Information

Calories................................ 68
Total Fat..............................<1g
Saturated Fat.....................<1g
Protein 1g
Carbohydrate....................17g
Cholesterol.....................0mg
Fiber.......................................2g
Sodium............................13mg

Dietary Exchanges:
1½ Vegetable, ½ Fruit

Black Bean Stuffed Peppers
(page 183)

Recipe Index

Recipe Index

Recipe Index

Recipe Index

Recipe Index

Recipe Index

Metric Chart

VOLUME MEASUREMENTS (dry)

¹/₈ teaspoon = 0.5 mL
¹/₄ teaspoon = 1 mL
¹/₂ teaspoon = 2 mL
³/₄ teaspoon = 4 mL
1 teaspoon = 5 mL
1 tablespoon = 15 mL
2 tablespoons = 30 mL
¹/₄ cup = 60 mL
¹/₃ cup = 75 mL
¹/₂ cup = 125 mL
²/₃ cup = 150 mL
³/₄ cup = 175 mL
1 cup = 250 mL
2 cups = 1 pint = 500 mL
3 cups = 750 mL
4 cups = 1 quart = 1 L

VOLUME MEASUREMENTS (fluid)

1 fluid ounce (2 tablespoons) = 30 mL
4 fluid ounces (¹/₂ cup) = 125 mL
8 fluid ounces (1 cup) = 250 mL
12 fluid ounces (1¹/₂ cups) = 375 mL
16 fluid ounces (2 cups) = 500 mL

WEIGHTS (mass)

¹/₂ ounce = 15 g
1 ounce = 30 g
3 ounces = 90 g
4 ounces = 120 g
8 ounces = 225 g
10 ounces = 285 g
12 ounces = 360 g
16 ounces = 1 pound = 450 g

DIMENSIONS

¹/₁₆ inch = 2 mm
¹/₈ inch = 3 mm
¹/₄ inch = 6 mm
¹/₂ inch = 1.5 cm
³/₄ inch = 2 cm
1 inch = 2.5 cm

OVEN TEMPERATURES

250°F = 120°C
275°F = 140°C
300°F = 150°C
325°F = 160°C
350°F = 180°C
375°F = 190°C
400°F = 200°C
425°F = 220°C
450°F = 230°C

BAKING PAN AND DISH EQUIVALENTS

Utensil	Size in Inches	Size in Centimeters	Volume	Metric Volume
Baking or Cake Pan (square or rectangular)	8×8×2	20×20×5	8 cups	2 L
	9×9×2	23×23×5	10 cups	2.5 L
	13×9×2	33×23×5	12 cups	3 L
Loaf Pan	8¹/₂×4¹/₂×2¹/₂	21×11×6	6 cups	1.5 L
	9×9×3	23×13×7	8 cups	2 L
Round Layer Cake Pan	8×1¹/₂	20×4	4 cups	1 L
	9×1¹/₂	23×4	5 cups	1.25 L
Pie Plate	8×1¹/₂	20×4	4 cups	1 L
	9×1¹/₂	23×4	5 cups	1.25 L
Baking Dish or Casserole			1 quart/4 cups	1 L
			1¹/₂ quart/6 cups	1.5 L
			2 quart/8 cups	2 L
			3 quart/12 cups	3 L